Fresh Flowers

IDENTIFYING, SELECTING, AND ARRANGING

CHARLES MARDEN FITCH

Fresh Flowers

IDENTIFYING, SELECTING, AND ARRANGING

ABBEVILLE PRESS, PUBLISHERS
NEW YORK   LONDON   PARIS

Editor: Susan Costello
Designer: Nai Y. Chang
Production Supervisor: Hope Koturo
Copy Chief: Robin James
Editorial Assistant: Karel Birnbaum
Illustrators: Bobbi Angell, Dolores
Santoliquido

First edition.

Library of Congress Cataloging-in-Publication Data

Fitch, Charles Marden.
Fresh flowers: identifying, selecting, and arranging /
Charles Marden Fitch. —1st ed.
p. cm.
Includes bibliographical references (p.) and index.
ISBN 1-55859-217-2
1. Cut flowers. 2. Cut flowers—Identification. 3. Cut
foliage. 4. Flower arrangement. I. Title.
SB449.F525 1992
745.92—dc20   91-48003
                                     CIP

Dedication

This book is dedicated to all of the professionals whose orientation is international and who make our lives richer with fresh flowers. Our joy begins with collectors discovering exceptional plants, continues to hybridizers, growers, shippers, wholesalers, retailers, and, of course, talented designers creating innovative arrangements with fresh flowers. To all of these floraculture professionals, congratulations for your dedication and talent.

A Note About the Photo Selection

Abbeville's creative staff and I spent many hours selecting the photographs for this volume. I believe the final choices represent the variety and beauty of cut-flower types available in florists, markets, or even in your own garden or greenhouse. We have tried to include superior examples of fresh flowers as well as a wide range of the best foliage selections. A few less common flowers and leaves are also shown, enriching the book's scope. With the correct names at hand you can order these flowers and foliage from your local florist.

Credits

Photographs: All are by the author unless otherwise credited.
Illustrations: All drawings are by Bobbi Angell except the orchids by Dolores Santoliquido on pages 224, 226, 229–30, 232, 241–44, 248.

Author's Note

Flowers have always been an enriching part of my life. My father, a physician, found relaxation and renewal in our garden, teaching me by example the joys of nature's world. Mother was the first to show me how much fun it is to arrange flowers and nurture houseplants.

The first design I ever created won a grand prize in my fifth-grade show-and-tell contest. Since that joyful event decades ago I have learned firsthand how flowers are grown and loved around the world.

In Colombia, during two years as a television director/producer with the United States Peace Corps, I studied flowers on Andean peaks, in rich valleys, and in humid Amazonian jungles. Later, many explorations of Southeast Asia taught me about orchids, aroids, and countless tropical treasures. Assignments and research around the world help me understand ecology and horticulture in varied habitats.

Living close to nature—be it a single rose or a room filled with orchids—enriches the spirit. Living indoor plants, such natural companions to fresh cut flowers, keep our air clean and moist. This book is designed to bring fresh flowers into your daily life—to help you find excitement and pleasure from an international world of fresh flowers.

CONTENTS

INTRODUCTION

Fresh flowers are not only a welcome source of color, fragrance, and grace but also an important element in ceremonies, celebrations, and festivals around the world. Friends and lovers exchange flowers in gestures of affection; places of worship are often decorated with flowers—from marigolds at Hindu shrines through orchids in Buddhist temples to altar flowers in Christian churches. Gracious homes, hotels, and offices are decorated with fresh flowers. Parades, weddings, parties, even funerals feature flowers. Nature's beauty lifts our spirits. Emotional moments are all the more important when we are surrounded with living beauty.

As a gardener, I love flowers outdoors; but I never hesitate to pick them for intimate indoor enjoyment. Seeing flowers close up lets us appreciate their intricate detail, fragrances, and combined charms. If you are fortunate enough to have a source of fresh flowers in a garden, greenhouse, or an indoor plant collection, you, too, have a personal array of decorative flowers and leaves. I enjoy combining plants from my collection with exotic flowers from florists. Even people who grow their own flowers turn to international sources for special arrangements and important occasions.

While gardeners have the privilege of cultivating beautiful plants, everyone can enjoy the bounty. Thanks to modern air transportation, fresh flowers are available in most cities of the world throughout the year. You can even order some flowers directly from wholesaler shippers or growers, for delivery to your door via U.P.S., Federal Express, or other shipping services.

How do you get the best? A basic understanding of how flowers reach us will help you find the freshest and most appealing flowers.

Above. On a sheer cliff 600 feet above the tropical plains in Sigiriya, Sri Lanka, this fifth century fresco depicts a royal lady offering lotus buds and a fragrant Champac flower (*Michelia* sp.) to Buddha. In modern Ceylon, now Sri Lanka, both flowers are still favorite offerings.

Opposite. In Thailand hand-tailored lotus buds are frequently offered as altar decorations at Buddhist temples.

7

In Amsterdam (top) on Saturday mornings the flower market features fairly priced flowers.

At Holland's Aalsmeer auction (above) flowers arrive from around the world for immediate sale and reshipping. Here roses rest in buckets of preservative solution. Electric carts pull long trains filled with flowers through temperature-controlled rooms, conveying them from the seller to the buyer to the shipper.

International Trade

Fresh flower growers around the world sell their products in three major ways: in local markets, via direct export, and in international avenues. As a rule, the greatest volume of sales is not where the flowers are raised, but in the direct exports to large wholesale markets. Cartons of carnations, for example, are sent from Colombia to California, while roses go from Mexico to New York, anthuriums from Hawaii to Japan, and sprays of dendrobium orchids from Thailand to Europe and the United States.

Aalsmeer Auction

The world's largest international flower auction center is Aalsmeer, in The Netherlands. Commercial growers in South America, Asia, Australia, Israel, and Europe sell some of their fresh products to the world-famous Dutch auctions. Aalsmeer is a model of efficiency for bringing floral beauty to the world. Specially designed tubs ensure freshness—they hold floral preservative around the stems of freshly cut flowers. Many cut flowers sold through the Dutch auctions are shipped right in these tubs, and remain there until they are sold by importers thousands of miles away.

In 1912 two Dutch cooperatives, Bloemenlust Flower Auction and Centrale Aalsmeer Auction, began working together in selling plant products. In the 1920s both cooperatives flourished, and after the Second World War, expanded international trade and improved transportation brought renewed prosperity. By 1968 both cooperatives merged into the present Aalsmeer Flower Auction, which accounted for roughly one-third of all Dutch exports of cut flowers in 1990.

The Aalsmeer Flower Auction buildings cover an area larger than 90 football fields or 630,000 square meters. Buyers work in new auction halls with 13 electronic bidding clocks, and more than 12.6 million cut flowers are purchased every day. An average of 80 percent of these flowers are then exported, many by refrigerated trucks to nearby European countries, others by jet planes to wholesale markets around the world.

The auction members, originally all Dutch growers, now include growers and exporters from many flower-producing countries. The growers find that the auction is the least expensive and most efficient way to sell their highly perishable products. Foreign suppliers contribute about 16 percent of the flowers sold at Aalsmeer.

International Flower Village

Cut flowers are flown into Aalsmeer from such diverse locales as Australia, Colombia, Greece, Israel, Italy, Kenya, Singapore, Thailand, the United States, and Zimbabwe. In the Aalsmeer auction complex, 310 wholesalers and exporters have offices and flower preparation areas. Under the same acres of roof are restaurants, banks, consulting services, agricultural inspection services and vast temperature-controlled areas for holding fresh flowers. Buyers, using state-of-the-art electronic bidding controls, bid on products they want. Orders are transferred to shipping clerks, who soon speed the flowers on to wholesalers, makers of bouquets, and retail florists.

International shipments are usually sold by a wholesaler who takes the responsibility of picking up the boxes from customs at major airports, inspects for damage, handles flowers with professional care, and finally sends off orders to the retail shop or local wholesalers.

Flower auctions, filled with fresh imports, play an important role in distributing beauty. Thanks to many international suppliers, and the Dutch talent for growing crops in greenhouses, we can enjoy many flowers all year around. Tulips and roses, for example, are no longer just spring and summer flowers. Orchids, once very expensive and difficult to find, are now common in cut-flower markets.

Recently the Westland auction complex between Rotterdam and The Hague merged with the Flower Auction Berkel in Bleiswijk forming a new cooperative, Flower Auction Holland. The new alliance has 4,300 growers, 2,100 buyers, and 1,700 auction employees. Flower auctions

At the Los Angeles flower market, snapdragons, tuberoses, delphiniums, and alstroemerias arrive in water tubs from Holland's Aalsmeer auction. With their stems in a preservative solution, the flowers remain in excellent condition, even after international travel.

have now been established in other places, such as San Diego, California, and Vancouver, British Columbia. The Vancouver flower auction is the largest in North America with recent yearly sales of $25 million. The Dutch still lead in export volume and value.

The Flower Council of Holland reports that Holland supplies 70 percent of the world's cut flowers—in 1990, nearly 9 billion stems of fresh flowers were sold through Dutch auctions.

A Constant Supply

Raising flowers is important to the economies of many countries. In The Netherlands, about 70,000 people are employed in the flori-cultural industry, over 11,000 as growers under glass and outdoors. In some developing nations, the cash crops of fresh flowers are vital: in Colombia, for example, there are more than 3,000 flower growers and

Orchids on sale at the Los Angeles flower market include cattleyas, paphiopedilums, and odontoglossum hybrids, each with stems in water-filled tubes.

Modern hybrid carnations thrive in Colombia's rich Andean soil and cool, moist sabanas, or valleys, providing an abundant supply of flowers for export primarily to the United States.

100,000 families who make incomes from the flower trade.

In the case of Colombia, about 83 percent of the fresh flowers are exported to the United States. In 1990 Colombia supplied about 11 percent of the world's cut flowers. Growing a superior crop and having a constant supply is vital to suppliers of cut flowers. Because of advanced tissue culture and propagation techniques, growers can reproduce thousands of plants from a single superior individual (or clone).

Now growers can offer crops of precise characteristics at desired seasons. The most successful grower/owners travel from their farms to international exhibitions each year, searching for improved plants. Hybridizers, producers of tissue culture, and wholesale plant growers all compete for the attention of cut flower growers by creating elaborate displays of new flowers and pot plants. Growers, in turn, order plants, seeds, bulbs, tissue culture plantlets or other propagations, and then rush to get a cut flower crop to market.

Your benefits from these developments are a wide selection of superior fresh cut flowers. Growers now cultivate selections with increased flower count, clearer colors, desired shapes, good shipping durability, and long vase life. By cultivating blocks of several thousand identical plants, the growers can meet our demands with a superior living product.

I.
SELECTING THE BEST:
How to Buy Flowers

Getting the best in cut flowers begins with knowing what to look for. While freshness is the most important requirement, even just-picked flowers can have a short life if they are not treated correctly or picked at the optimum stage. Besides freshness and good timing for harvest, you should be looking for quality in shape, color, and condition. The most beautiful orchid, kept nicely fresh with a stem water tube, is not much to look at if the petals are bruised or the shape distorted by poor packing techniques.

In chapter 2 you will find suggestions for helping fresh flowers and foliage last. How long your flowers remain fresh is related to how they were grown, harvested, shipped, and held before arriving at your home. A few basic factors prolong flower life. These affect the typical cut life of hybrids and cultivars and include harvesting at the optimum stage of development; cool, moist conditions immediately following harvest; suitable temperatures and rapid transport from field to sales outlet; conditioning with appropriate solutions by grower; and holding in fresh floral preservative solutions or pure water. Factors that can shorten the life of cut flowers include: dry heat or freezing temperatures; direct sun; ethylene gas; and fluoride in water. In addition, exposure of stems to sap from freshly cut daffodils can shorten a flower's life. Some hybrids and

Above.
Cattleya Irene Holguin was grown at Stewart Orchids in California, a supplier of prize-winning cut flowers.

Opposite.
Liatris 'Callilepis' (top), and China asters, with foxglove in the background (bottom), stay fresh in wholesalers' cool, humid rooms.

13

Sweet William
(*Dianthus barbatus*) hybrids are especially valued for their pleasant fragrance.

cultivars have comparatively short-lived flowers. And, of course, poor handling by growers, shippers, or sellers will have a bad effect.

Gerberas are best picked after the two innermost rows of petals have opened, as shown here.

Ultrafresh Blossoms

The freshest flowers you can find will come from your own garden—whether it is an outdoor garden or an indoor growing area. (Even if you live in an apartment you can have a garden under fluorescent lights or at a window.)

The second freshest flowers will come from local growers. Suburban

Gerberas are shipped without water under cool, moist conditions in cartons that have been specially designed to protect the flowers from being crushed. The shipping trays are often set over buckets of water (top) to give them a long drink after their trip from grower to wholesaler. In contrast, some wholesale markets (above) simply display gerberas with dry stems, because these popular flowers will be sold quickly.

and rural areas are likely to have farmers' markets and local stands offering daily fresh flowers grown in nearby fields and greenhouses.

No matter how careful overseas shippers are in jetting their flowers to our markets, the flowers still have to endure a few days of travel and possible shipping damage, so locally grown flowers are better. Even in larger cities you can still find fresh local flowers at florists who welcome supplies that come to their shops free of jet lag.

The most careful suppliers of fresh flowers use specially constructed shipping boxes designed for each crop. Orchids, for example, are generally tough, long-lasting flowers. In my own collection I grow hundreds of tropical orchids that produce perfect flowers which last for weeks when cut. But because the flower structure is complex, each bloom is subject to damage when shipped. Orchids travel well if picked when ripe, kept at a moderate temperature with water tubes on each stem, and cushioned during shipping. Cattleya orchids may travel in heavy cardboard boxes designed to hold individual water tubes in fixed positions so no flower gets crushed. Gerberas are packed with each flower in a spaced hole and anthuriums are packed with individual flower covers and careful layering in cartons designed for such crops. Beware of orchids that are shipped without padding between the stems and flowers.

What is more, even well-designed shipping boxes may be filled with several layers of orchid bundles. After a day at the bottom of such a box, the orchids get so crushed that they never regain their proper form. Similar damage can occur to anthurium spathes, which once bent or cracked never look well. It is helpful to study a flower's structure before making a purchase.

Evaluating Quality

When you select flowers, use the same care you would in selecting fresh produce. Check petal substance for shrinking and discoloration. Fresh flowers have firm petals, and no shrink marks, curling, brown edges, or fungus (Botrytis) spots. Colors should be clear and bright, appropriate

Flexible net socks may be used to protect gerbera hybrids during shipping. After the socks are gently removed, each flower should open perfectly.

This delphinium (above) may look fresh from a distance but close inspection reveals mold, a consequence of stuffy, moist shipping or storage.

Another example of flowers that have passed their prime are these Dutch irises (right), which have dry bud tips and yellowing leaves.

to the variety. With multiflowered stems, choose those with no more than three-quarters of the flowers open. Reject wilted, wrinkled, bruised specimens, and choose instead bright, firm, unblemished offerings. Top-quality fresh flowers have straight, sturdy, firm stems. Poor-quality roses and gerberas show drooping stems quickly as they age, and many old flowers have shrunken, discolored, or slimy stems.

Check the charts on flower types in the appendices for basic information on harvest time and the optimum ripeness for cutting of different flowers. In general, choose flowers that are already at least half open. Tight buds and buds without color showing seldom develop once stems are cut from the plant. In the case of potted (growing) flowering plants, such as orchids, azaleas, lilies, begonias, miniature roses, and hibiscus, small buds are acceptable.

For most flower purchases you will want ultrafresh specimens at a fair market price. You can help guarantee long vase life by making your choice carefully. Look for firm petals, clear color, and clean foliage.

Unlike the flowers shown on the opposite page, these top quality fresh flowers—Chrysanthemum 'Grenadine'—display good color and buds that have just opened.

19

Firm petals, clear colors, and clean foliage are characteristics of these *Ranunculus asiaticus* hybrids of the Tecolote strain, which also offer double flowers.

Study stems, especially those packed in plastic or under water, to detect signs of decay. Poor-quality cut flowers often have slimy stems and foliage that has begun to rot. If you need fresh flowers only for a single event, such as a dinner party, you might save money by searching for fully ripe flowers marked down in price. Roses, for example, look lushly beautiful just before the petals drop; fully open lilies are glorious but difficult to pack and soon drop their petals. Just as the produce manager has a table of marked-down, fully ripe fruit for fast sale, so too you may get good prices on fully ripe, fresh-cut flowers. If you do buy mature flowers, however, remember that they usually last only a day or two.

Be especially careful when buying flowers just before major holidays. Growers are known to put cut blooms into cold storage, saving them for release when prices are highest. Such practices result in flowers that are guaranteed not to last well.

Smart florists discard stale flowers and slimy stalks before the public even sees them. Wholesale distributors credit florists with refunds or replacements when their fresh products are below acceptable quality. Some old flowers still get sold, usually on the street or at discount prices elsewhere.

Foliage on flowers past their prime will be yellowish or brown, perhaps curled. Alstroemerias, carnations, and lilies soon show yellowing leaves when flowers age.

Evaluate cut flowers and foliage for physical damage such as bruising, cracking, crushing, tearing. Flowers that have been poorly cared for often show signs of mechanical damage. Even relatively tough flowers such as anthuriums and dendrobium orchids will be crushed when too many are layered in shipping cartons.

Potted plants are often a good alternative to cut flowers, especially around holidays. Given enough light and humidity, a growing potted plant will develop buds that provide pleasure for weeks. Most potted flowering plants come with tags outlining culture recommendations.

These good-quality carnations and yarrow are for sale at reduced prices because the flowers are fully ripe.

21

Good Sources Are Important

Search for florists who guarantee freshness. Most flower vendors, at wholesale and retail levels, will replace flowers that die much before their normal vase life. Many successful retail florists say they always resolve customer complaints about short-lived arrangements by replacing the fast-fading flowers. This is an excellent policy tailored to keeping customers.

Even at supermarkets, where conscientious managers sometimes fall behind on grooming their wares, the flower-department manager will often replace poor-quality, fast-fading flowers if you return the unsatisfactory goods as evidence. Flowers purchased from mall kiosks, machines, and at some supermarkets, however, often have no such personal backing. If you look carefully at flower vending machines you can find a phone number for registering complaints.

Personal Delivery

You can order flowers from distant places for personal delivery to your door. Thanks to professional packing and speedy delivery, most flower shipments will get to you in perfect condition, perhaps even better than poorly cared for flowers offered in markets! Most such deliveries are handled by private carriers that offer one- or two-day service.

When receiving fresh flowers by mail order, open the carton immediately. Check for signs of damage, such as freezing in cold weather, extreme wilting in hot weather, crushing, discoloration, and bruising. The best vendors of fresh shipped flowers will replace flowers that arrive in poor condition. Notify the carrier if you find any damage. Sometimes insurance and replacement guarantees require immediate reporting of damage, and you may be asked to hold damaged goods for inspection.

Also look for any discrepancy between your original order and what has actually been received. Remember that some shippers reserve the right (check their catalogs or ads) to vary flowers sent, according to season, crop, and quality. Often a substitution is made (of one color for another, for example) in order to ensure the best quality. If you must have a very precise color or type, be sure to say so when ordering.

Wire Delivery Services

Florist wire delivery services offer the convenience of choosing specific designs at a florist near you when the actual arrangement or cut stems will be delivered in a distant city. Thus you can choose the style and general ingredients of an arrangement for a friend across the country or in another country. Your local florist, using wire service connections, sends the order to an approved florist in your chosen city of delivery.

Flowers sent by wire are slightly more costly than locally purchased ones because florists usually charge for long-distance costs. Florists often belong to more than one wire service. The major services in the United States are American Floral Services (AFS), the cooperative Florist's Transworld Delivery Association (FTD), Florafax, and Teleflora.

Wire services all offer benefits to member florists, including design training, business seminars, and international connections to expand sales. With several wire services to choose from you will have an easy time sending or receiving fresh flowers from almost anywhere. These services have comprehensive quality-control programs, including test ordering procedures to evaluate member florist products. Customer satisfaction is a priority. In the unlikely event that an order is unsatisfactory, both the florist and wire service will work to resolve the problem, usually by making an immediate replacement.

The so-called Cleopatra vase of plastic-coated paper comes flat but may be opened to hold water, thus providing a practical container for displaying bouquets that are shipped, such as this assortment of miniature carnations.

2.
PRESERVING BEAUTY:
Helping Fresh Flowers Last

How long fresh-cut flowers last depends on the care given each stem, from the time it is removed from a growing plant until the fresh material appears in your arrangement. Florists call this progression of care the "Chain of Life."

General Principles

The best care may vary with different types of flowers and foliage, but fortunately some basic rules apply to all fresh material. (If your fresh flowers come from a commercial source they may have already been given some care, including chemical preservative solutions. Alternatively, many florists include a packet of floral preservative with every purchase. Ask the vendor what treatments have been given to the flowers and foliage you buy from a commercial source.) The steps listed below are intended for plant material you have gathered yourself.

1. Harvest flowers and foliage when the material is cool and will have had all night to replace water lost during the day. The second best time to harvest is very late in the afternoon, after the plants have cooled down.
2. Use sharp shears, a serrated knife, or flower-cutting snips to harvest. Ordinary scissors may crush stems, and dull shears make

Above. This tool caddy is useful for holding bottles of water when collecting cut flowers in the garden. Fresh flowers are more likely to last if their stems are plunged into water seconds after gathering them.

Opposite. A curly willow branch supports tall stems of bold Germini gerberas, creating a striking design. An antique morter filled with fragrant potpourri adds another dimension to this 24-inch-tall arrangement. When flowers have no perfume of their own, your favorite potpourri may be added to provide an aura of fragrance.

ragged cuts. Cut stems on an angle to provide maximum area for water absorption.

3. Immediately after cutting, plunge stems under several inches of lukewarm water. I carry a bucket or sturdy vase with me into the garden so each stem can be put in water quickly. Adding a flower preservative to the water will further increase flower life. (See step number 6.)

4. Put cut material in a cool, shady, fairly humid place (at least 50 percent relative humidity) until you are ready to create your arrangement.

5. If the flowers or foliage are dirty or wilting, give them a gentle shower under lukewarm water, then put the stems back into fresh water.

6. Mix a flower preservative with the water for maximum life of cut material. Flower preservatives provide sugar to help buds open, an acid material to make water less hospitable to bacteria, and often a chemical to further retard bacteria growth. Bacteria speed decay of plant stems and can restrict water absorption by clogging stems.

7. Remove all leaves that would otherwise be below water in the final arrangement. Under water, foliage rots quickly, shortening flower life by fouling the water, clogging stems, and raising levels of harmful ethylene gas.

Carnations (top left) should be cut between stem nodes, as shown here. Dahlias (far left) will be long-lived if they are soaked from six to twelve hours in a cool location before arranging.

The lilac in plain water, at left, has begun to droop while the same variety, at its right, in a Chrysal flower preservative solution, still has a nice appearance.

8. Just before placing flowers in an arrangement, cut the stems once more, under water. I use a big bowl of warm water, or fill up the whole sink if I have many long stems to cut. Cutting under water lets the stem absorb liquid rather than air. Once you make an initial cut under water you can lift the stems out to make arrangements. Water clinging to stem ends will restrict air absorption.

9. Keep flowers away from smoke, heat, and fruit.

Ideal Temperatures

Cool temperatures prolong flower life by slowing biological processes. At cool temperatures, buds open more slowly and deterioration is discouraged. How cool a temperature should be depends on the flowers at hand.

The best florists maintain two coolers—tropical and temperate; each has high humidity (90 to 95 percent) but a different temperature range suited to different plant types. Flowers and foliage of temperate-climate plants keep well at 32° to 43° F (0° to 6° C). This temperature range is common for carnations, iris, roses, snapdragons, and most of the commonly used foliage greens. At home you can fashion a reasonable equivalent of these ideal storage conditions in an empty vegetable compartment of your refrigerator. Clear away nearby vegetables and fruits, which give off harmful ethylene gas. Wash the vegetable box with a household bleach solution; then dry it and line the bottom with clean, moist towels (paper or cotton). Now the clean humid compartment is a safe place to store flowers that prefer cooler temperatures.

Tropical flowers and foliage need moderate, not cold, temperatures to last best. A range of 55° to 60° F (13° to 15° C) is fine for callas, orchids, gingers, birds of paradise, heliconias, and similar warmth-loving blooms. Caladium and alocasia leaves, which are easily damaged by cool temperatures, do best at 60° to 65° F.

Gerberas are susceptible to drooping stems (top). To delay this process some growers and florists wind thin wire around each flower stem (above). The wire keeps the necks straight even when the stems fail to absorb adequate water.

Arrangements for special events often must be made a day or two in advance. Florists keep designs fresh in large, humid walk-in coolers, here filled with designs by Lorraine Roxbury.

Tropicals kept too cool may discolor. Use a thermometer to determine temperatures in your home refrigerator; the lower shelves are generally the warmer ones. The tropicals last best with high humidity; under home conditions, 50 to 60 percent relative humidity is reasonable, but florists use 90 to 95 percent for maximum storage life.

If your flowers will be on display in a dry place, mist them in the morning and the afternoon. Flowers such as anthuriums and gardenias, which take up little water once cut, benefit greatly from misting. Avoid having water accumulate in bracts or pouches of flowers that have these waterholding sections, such as some heliconias, gingers, and paphiopedilum orchids. Standing water encourages rot.

More Advanced Treatments

In addition to the general steps listed above you can give some flowers and foliage special treatment tailored to their individual needs. The following are the most useful special treatments. Refer to the genus discussions in the last section of the book to find which steps are appropriate for each flower type.

ANTITRANSPIRANT SPRAY

Many thick leaves and evergreens such as conifers will last longer when given a thin coating of antitranspirant spray. The coating greatly reduces water loss (transpiration) from the foliage and it adds a nice glossy wet look. I spray holly and conifer branches with Wilt-Pruf antitranspirant before using them in an arrangement.

Foliage oils and shine solutions also reduce water loss from leaf pores. Tropical specialist David Carli at Costa Flores provides designers with a light white oil labeled "Jungle Juice," a lightly scented mineral oil. Mr. Carli recommends that tropical foliage such as croton and ti leaves be lightly coated with the "Jungle Juice." The treatment provides a glossy look while helping to retain moisture in the colorful leaves.

BOILING WATER

Dip cut stems several inches into a pan of boiling water for 30 to 60 seconds. The hot water kills some bacteria that contribute to decay and fosters the flow of water into stems. Dahlias, snapdragons, clematis, ferns, gerberas—in fact most of the fresh material used in arrangements benefit from such a dip.

CAUTERIZING STEM ENDS

You can stop the sap flow in a flower stem by holding the cut stem in a flame until it begins to turn black. This quick singe is useful for poppies, euphorbias, and other plants with thick milky sap that clogs stems and fouls water.

FILLING STEMS

Hollow stems, such as those of amaryllises and delphiniums, can be filled with water, then plugged up with wet cotton or a chunk of floral foam. Doing this removes the air barrier inside a stem, ensuring that it will

Top. *Helleborus orientalis* lasts longer when freshly cut stems are dipped for 30 seconds in boiling water (right). In contrast, the stem at left received no treatment.

Above. After three days the clematis at left shows that a stem dip in hot water does help flowers endure. The faded flower at right received no treatment.

Left. After cutting, the stem of a Rose 'Perfect Moment', at left, was dipped in boiling water for 30 seconds while nothing was done to the stem at right.

continue to absorb water when you put the flowers back in a vase or bowl of water.

IMMERSION

A good way to restore anthuriums, dendrobium orchids, and tropical foliage that have been in transit is to give them a total soak, with stems and flowers under water. Even freshly harvested flowers last longer if soaked in warm water for 15 minutes. Caladium expert Terri Bates recommends that caladium leaves be soaked overnight to make the stems stronger. Immersing foliage and flowers even for a short while is also a good way to be sure they are clean before placing them in arrangements.

WOOD-ALCOHOL STEM DIP

Recent research shows that poinsettias last longest when the cut stems are given a 10-minute soak in a 95 percent solution of wood alcohol. I did a simple test, however, and found flower bracts on untreated stems lasted longer than any of the treatments.

Professional Chemical Treatments

Florists and professional growers often treat their crops chemically before the flowers are sold. These treatments, which involve chemicals that should be handled with great care, are routine for some commercial cut flowers, including those sold at the Aalsmeer auction for export. The popular professional treatments given by large-scale wholesale growers and shippers are listed below. You can, with careful handling, adapt some of these treatments for home use.

PULSE TREATMENTS

Freshly cut stems are plunged in solutions of sucrose and citric acid. The sucrose helps flower buds develop; citric acid creates an acid condition that helps stems absorb water.

Commercial growers often add biocides—chemicals to discourage bacteria—to pulsing solutions. At home you can mix ¼ teaspoon household bleach with 1 gallon of warm water to make a solution that discourages bacterial growth. For succulent stems that decay fast (such as allium or stock), use ½ teaspoon of bleach per gallon of water. The disinfectant Physan 20, popular with orchid growers to control Botrytis, petal spotting, and algae, is useful in flower water to restrain bacterial growth. Use I teaspoon of Physan 20 per gallon of water in flower vases, tubes, or foams.

SILVER THIOSULFATE (STS)

Flowers sensitive to ethylene gas (including alstroemerias, carnations, and roses, among others) are given a soak or spray of silver thiosulfate solution to protect them from premature wilting. The STS treatment also helps buds develop and retards shattering of some flowers such as calceolarias and snapdragons. The STS treatment is designed for application by trained professionals and is not recommended for home use.

HYDRATING

This treatment, which helps flowers to absorb water, is done by florists to restore flowers after shipping or after dry storage. Most florists soak stems in a solution of warm water with a wetting agent and acidifier such as citric acid. Soaking times vary from several hours to overnight. I like to soak woody stems, roses, bouvardias, and carnations overnight in a cool shady place before arranging them.

PRESERVATIVE SOLUTIONS

Growers, shippers, and florists may all use preservative solutions to keep flowers in good condition between field and retail consumer. Preservative solutions include professional formulations of biocides, acidifiers, and a sugar ingredient.

Nonprofessionals should use a prepared floral preservative powder designed to be dissolved in water. Popular brands include Chrysal, Floralife, and Oasis Floral Preservative. Vitabric is a preservative mixed into a 2-inch label (Keri Blooms) that is designed to be placed in a vase of water with the flowers. The manufacturer recommends adding I teaspoon of plain sugar to each pint of solution. The sugar furnishes food to help buds develop.

If you wish to make your own version of flower preservative, mix the

Top. The STS label on a box of carnations from Colombia shows that the exporter treated freshly cut stems with silver thiosulfate to increase the flower life.

Above. Floral preservative powders in water prolong the lives of flowers. Many florists include a packet of preservatives with their flowers.

Opposite. While these poinsettia stems (top) received different treatments after cutting, all looked equally lovely for fifteen days. To stop the flow of sap quickly (center) from freshly cut poinsettias, it is best to singe the stem under a flame. Sixteen days after various stem treatments (bottom), poinsettias begin to show differences. The best flowers are on the stem given no treatment.

following in 1 gallon of warm water: ¼ to ½ teaspoon household bleach, ¼ teaspoon citric acid (from drugstore or florist supply company), and 3 teaspoons sugar.

Water Quality

One of the most important factors in the vase life of fresh flowers is the composition of the water you will use. The pH (acid-alkaline) balance in tap water varies from place to place. Flowers absorb water best when the water is acid—with a pH rating of 3.5 being ideal. Very alkaline ("hard") water needs more floral preservative to make it acid enough for good water absorption. Acid water also slows the growth of stem-clogging bacteria and molds. Too much or too little preservative can shorten flower life. Smither-Oasis and Floralife companies offer a water-quality analysis to florists in an effort to maximize the positive results of preservative solutions. An analysis of your water can be very helpful. On the basis of one such test, I learned that my municipal water was very low in dissolved mineral salts, relatively pure, and slightly acid. The lab technician thus recommended that I use only ⅓ ounce (about 2 teaspoons) of preservative powder per gallon. The average quantity, printed on package directions, is 1⅓ ounces per gallon.

If you find stems rotting in a few days, even though you are using a flower preservative, check the pH of your water. Acid water requires less preservative, alkaline water needs more.

Many municipalities add fluoride to community water supplies to reduce tooth decay. Some flowers, however, such as gerberas and roses, develop discoloration or water spots in water that has too much fluoride. Up to 4 parts per million of fluoride may be found in drinking water, but as little as 2 parts per million can shorten the life of roses. If your water causes problems with cut flowers because of fluoride, use spring water.

Dissolved Salts

Flowers do not last as well in water with a high concentration of dissolved mineral salts. Some parts of Florida, for example, have such a high concentration of salts in well or municipal water that florists and plant growers must use deionized water, rainwater, or water that has been run through a reverse-osmosis device. Orchid plants are especially prone to root damage from high salt content in the water.

The Floralife company offers three blends of flower preservative so florists can tailor preservative formulas to their water supply. A blend called "Pure Water" is best in purified water. The universal formula is suitable "for the vast majority of typical waters." This broad category excludes waters of extreme purity and those of high alkalinity and high salt levels. For very alkaline water and high salt levels the "Hard Water" Floralife blend works best.

Special Tips for Roses

Researchers at Rutgers University have shown that cut roses are especially sensitive to high salt levels. Some floral foams contain mineral-salt residues that can reduce the life of cut roses. To minimize rose problems, researchers recommend that floral foams be saturated with floral preservative, not plain water, for use with roses.

When possible, use vases deep enough to cover the foam with solution. In this way, you get precise design control, yet the stems will always be covered by adequate solution. Flush saturated foam with floral preservative until the liquid runs freely through the material. This flushing will remove much of any salt concentrations in the foam.

Reviving Wilted Flowers

It is often possible to revive wilted flowers if you proceed before the stems are too far gone. Of the most popular fresh flowers, tulips, roses, and gerberas are likely to wilt the most. To revive sagging stems, snip off ½ inch, preferably under water, then plunge the flowers up to their necks in lukewarm water about 100° F.

Place your arrangement directly underneath a strong light source so

Above.
This display of roses, fern, and foxtail (*Asparagus densiflorus* 'Meyers') comes with Vitabric stickers and tags that have flower care hints as well as preservative. To make a preservative solution, the tags must be immersed in water.

Opposite.
These photos of gerberas reveal how they lasted after standing in solutions of water and various preservatives. The top photo shows gerberas at the start of this test, shortly after the stems were cut under warm water. After four days some of the gerberas (center) in three different preservative brands and a plain water control (right) begin to droop. There are dramatic differences after eleven days (bottom). The stems in Vita Flora preservative did best.

that the flowers will be oriented upward, rather than bent to the side. Gerberas with bent necks can be encouraged to look up if a strong light is kept above the flowers as the stems are soaking.

After two or three hours in a water soak, most wilted stems will revive. With tulips, you can further encourage water absorption and retard wilting by wrapping the bunches in damp newspaper before placing the stems in water.

Floral Foam

To supply water that will help flowers last while still providing support, many professionals use floral foam. (Chapter 6 covers other methods of mechanical support such as wire and pin holders.) Oasis, the original brand of floral foam, was developed by Vernon L. Smithers, who founded the Smither-Oasis Company of Kent, Ohio. Since its introduction in 1954, Oasis has become the best-known brand of floral foam.

Various flower arranging supplies include Oasis foams, water tubes, wires, and kenzan pin holders. Metal containers are fine for plain water but vases of glass, clay, or plastic are better for flowers in a preservative solution.

Foam blocks are offered in several formulations, each designed to do the best job with specific flowers. Oasis offers these five types of wettable floral foam:

Standard, for popular medium-sized flowers such as roses and chrysanthemums

Instant, a quickly saturating foam for people in a hurry

Deluxe, a heavier, denser foam for such thick-stemmed flowers as birds of paradise, gladiolus, and heliconias

Instant Deluxe, a dense foam with quick saturation qualities

Springtime, a foam for such delicate stems as daffodils, daisies, iris, and sweet peas

Using Foams

All floral foams saturate best when floated in warm water before use.

Oasis floral foam holders, candle adapters, and rings offer versatility to flower design. Orchids last best in small tubes of plain water, and these tubes can be pushed easily into floral foams if you wish to mix orchids with other flowers in a foam base.

Using Oasis foam in vacuum-stick "Place-It" holders, arrangements may be attached to such smooth surfaces as windows.

Drop the foam into a container filled with water or floral preservative (I prefer the latter) and let the foam float, absorbing water at its own rate. Keep adding water (or floral preservative solution) until the foam brick is totally saturated. Instant-type foams will be saturated in a few minutes, while the dense, heavy formulations may need 15 to 20 minutes before they are soaked through.

Cut foam with a sharp knife so it fits in whatever container you want to use; it is best to cut the foam after soaking. If dry foam is fitted too tightly into a container, it may not be able to saturate well. A square or rectangular block of foam is fine for use in a round container because it will leave space for water. If the foam fits very tightly, as in some square containers, cut off a corner or two of the foam to make space for reserve water.

For heavy arrangements, fasten foam blocks to the container bottom with double sided tape, putty, glue, or tacky florists' clay. You can also use a commercial foam holder designed to provide additional support.

Another way to secure foam bricks is to wrap them in 1- to 2-inch mesh chicken wire. Run a few strips of clear waterproof tape over the top of your container to further stabilize stems in very full or heavy arrangements, especially those that must be moved after you create them.

When inserting delicate stems into foam, grasp the stem low, just above the foam, while gently pushing it in. If the stem bends, which it often will, try making a preliminary hole in the foam with a stiff object slightly smaller than the stem to be inserted. (I like to use a thin bamboo skewer.)

Watering Flowers in Foam

Although floral foam does hold a great quantity of water, your arrangements will last best if the container has an additional reserve of water. Foam will furnish abundant water only if it is covered by the water or preservative solution. In any event be sure to keep the foam well soaked with flower preservative solution throughout the life of the arrangement. Push stems deeply into the foam, below the level of the reserve water supply in the container when possible.

With floral foam you can create an arrangement without a container. To minimize evaporation, wrap the foam block in aluminum foil or clear plastic wrap. Push stems through the foil or plastic wrap. It may be necessary to make an initial hole with a pencil tip or sharp stake.

Reusing and Storing Foam

Water-absorbing foam should only be used once if you want to insure maximum flower life. The foams are designed to surround the stem with liquid. Once the structure has been disturbed with multiple punctures, some stems may not receive adequate solution.

What is more, bacteria that cause decay can get a start even in arrangements treated with floral preservatives. Reusing wettable foam increases the chance that bacteria will quickly multiply in the foam and stems.

You may want to try reusing foam if your arrangements fade cleanly, without decay on the stems. In such a case pull out all of the old stems, wash the foam under hot water, removing any broken bits and adhering flower parts. Wrap the wet foam in plastic or put it in a waterproof plastic bag.

To decrease the chance that mold or bacteria will grow on stored wet foam, soak the foam in weak bleach (¼ teaspoon bleach per gallon of water) or spray it with a disinfectant spray. Once saturated, floral foam retains its structure better if kept wet.

Dry Flowers and Floral Foam

Floral foams also come in a form designed for dry flowers or silk flowers, sometimes called "permanent flowers." If you are making an arrangement only with dry stems or artificial flowers, insert the stems in nonabsorbent foam such as Oasis Sahara. Glue the foam brick into your container, wire it in place, or use tape to stabilize the arrangement.

These *Protea longiflora* hybrids and *Dryandra formosa* look attractive although they have been without water for a month. Sturdy proteas and related banksias and dryandra dry easily without any special treatments.

Glass marbles are useful at the base of flower designs to hold stems in place and to add weight. Wash marbles in strainers after each use.

When I combine fresh and dry stems I use the standard water-absorbing foams. After fresh flowers fade the dry stems take only a day or two to dry out again.

Reusing dry foams for dry or artificial flowers is practical. You may redesign the arrangement, store the dry foam for months, and keep using it until the multiple holes make design difficult.

Daily Care of Arrangements

Keeping water around stems is an important step in helping your cut-flower designs last. In general, the more a stem is covered with water the longer flowers will last. Flowers with stems several inches under water usually hold their good looks for two to three days longer than the same type of flower held in floral foam. I often use floral foam to hold stems in specific positions, perhaps even using some marbles on top of the foam to position stems further. With such an arrangement I always fill a container to the top, even if there is wet foam lower down in the vase.

A rubber bulb-type kitchen baster is useful for topping off narrow vases with water. Watering cans with long, thin spouts are handy for filling vases stuffed with flowers or for reaching into arrangements to top off water. Check the water supply every day. Some flowers, such as roses, absorb lots of water, while others hardly drink at all.

Anthuriums, daffodils, gingers, and other flowers that last better when misted can be misted every morning with pure plain water. Use a houseplant misting bottle or recycle your plastic spray bottles (be sure to give the empty container a good wash first with soapy water).

Check clear containers for water clarity every few days. If the water is cloudy, or if stems look mushy, dump out the old water or solution and refill with fresh floral preservative. If vase water looks dirty but the arrangement is too complex to move, just add a teaspoon of household bleach. The bleach will retard stem rot and bacteria growth.

Petal Protection

Some flowers, including chrysanthemums and dahlias, may drop some petals after a few days, especially when they are moved or shaken by a breeze. To minimize petal drop florists may spray the back side of flowers with a petal holding mist. You may find spray cans of "Mum Mist" or "Petal Proofer" at florist supply stores, or use extra-hold hair spray. Give the flowers a quick light mist at the back where petals join the stem.

Florists may also use clear glue to hold stems and flower parts. Using glue helps an arrangement endure during the rigors of delivery. Dabs of glue are popular in wedding bouquets because these flower creations receive much handling during the happy events. Cold glue is used with live flowers, while hot glue is helpful in decorating baskets and fastening dried materials. In your home arrangements glue should not be needed.

This design of larkspur, stock, and begonia leaves still looks nice after seven days, because it was kept out of the direct sun and the flowers were in a preservative solution.

3.
WHERE FRESH FLOWERS ARE GROWN:
The Art and Business of Flowers

With fresh flower selection the world really is a small place. Modern air and truck transportation speeds cut flowers from growers, through distribution channels, and on to retail outlets in cool, humid comfort. The fresh flowers in a bouquet from your local florist or supermarket were most likely grown in South America, Asia, Europe, and the United States. A rather basic arrangement can include roses from Mexico, chrysanthemums from Colombia, gypsophilas from California, ferns from Florida, and gerberas from Holland.

Science, Art, and Enthusiasm

In addition to those individuals who are responsible for transporting fresh flowers efficiently are the growers and hybridizers—people who devote their lives to developing sturdier, longer-lived, and ever more beautiful flowers. Floral beauty begins with dreams of plant breeders who work for years to develop the flowers we enjoy. Growers and plant explorers also contribute to the rich harvest by identifying new species that make good cut flowers.

New flower hybrids on display (opposite) at an international show in Holland include lilies, chrysanthemums, carnations, gerberas, alstroemerias, and euphorbias. Professional growers visit these shows to choose new crops for future cultivation.

In my travels around the world I enjoy interviewing plant hybridizers because their work is such a skillful blend of science and art. Big business is very much a part of modern cut-flower production, yet hybridizers and growers still retain their loving enthusiasm for nature.

To create improved cut flowers a hybridizer must be knowledgeable about each genus. Before any constructive hybridizing can begin, the plant breeder must know which species are compatible and what each is likely to contribute in a breeding program.

Breeding Boundaries

Hybridizers involved in creating superior flowers face certain breeding barriers; some of these limitations are dictated by nature, others by the interests of business. For example, cut flowers sell better when they have long, strong, straight stems. Clear flower colors and full petals have greater appeal than muddy hues and sparse forms. In breeding for the best characteristics in each genus, a hybridizer may be forced to compromise on some desired features. The most frequently sacrificed characteristic in cut flowers has been fragrance.

Old-fashioned roses, for example, usually have a distinct, strong fragrance. Most modern hybrids, however, have either no fragrance or a very mild perfume. The genetic road for full flowers, long strong stems, and bright clear colors takes a detour around the genes for fragrance. Modern hybrid roses thus have many desired characteristics of color, shape, and size, but the tendency toward heavy perfume is lost. Some of the most fragrant flowers have a shorter vase life than almost scentless selections. The same holds true for many modern carnations (*Dianthus*).

Another characteristic that sometimes gets lost in the competition for beauty is resistance to disease. A modern hybrid may have wonderful color and shape but be more susceptible to plant diseases than older, less highly bred strains. Growers may need to use more fungicides to keep the beautifully flowered modern hybrid healthy. It is always a joy when a recent hybrid exhibits not only improved color, form, and productivity but also improved disease resistance.

Making the Best Choice

How do growers choose their major flower crops—roses, chrysanthemums, carnations, tulips, lilies, freesias, and gerberas? Crop selection begins with hybridizers, many of whom specialize in one crop and develop improved hybrids for their commercial clients. Retail customers, designers, and florists do influence the process by their purchasing preferences.

When a hybridizer has a new plant ready for the marketplace, the chances of its success may still be slim. Commercial growers study new hybrids very carefully before making a commitment to plant them. Growing enough plants to produce a steady supply of cut flowers is a very costly investment in time, buildings, land, personnel, and all the other associated costs. Often a commercial grower will receive a few free test plants of a new hybrid, or buy just a few propagations to test. Only if the new plants produce well, on time, and with superior quality will a wise commercial grower make a decision to invest in thousands of plants.

Alstroemeria: *A Case Study*

Hybridizers frequently meet at international symposia to exchange ideas and learn about new developments. At a 1989 international symposium on bulbous plants, hybridizer Isamu Miyake from Japan told how his dream to develop a spotless alstroemeria was realized only after fourteen years of patient breeding experiments.

Why breed a spotless alstroemeria? Miyake explained: "Japanese people have a special preference for certain types of ornamental flowers. They prefer flowers which are simple and clear, while those with spots, stripes, or particular patterns have less market value. Therefore, one of the main goals in flower breeding is the elimination of undesirable characteristics."

Such a clearly stated goal is typical of hybridizers, even of those not working toward commercial sales. In my talks with managers at Van

Right and below.
Peruvian lilies *(Alstroemeria)* are popular, long-lasting cut flowers. These are some of the unique spotless Miyake hybrid alstroemerias developed in Japan. (Photographs courtesy of Isamu Miyake)

Opposite.
This ultrafresh display of white flowers (top) at the Amsterdam flower market includes chrysanthemums, stock, asters, and Baby's Breath *(Gypsophila)*.

At Van Staaveren company in Aalsmeer, Holland (center), professional hybridizers and growers test the vase life of new flowers. Here freesias and alstroemerias are being evaluated under conditions likely to be found in typical homes.

At the Van Staaveren facility (bottom), alstroemerias are grown from tissue cultured on agar in sterile dishes (foreground). Recently transplanted plantlets are in the background.

Staaveren in Holland, a leading breeder of ornamentals for cut flowers, I found that similar cultural preferences influence cut-flower sales in Europe. Van Staaveren's alstroemeria hybrids are available in individual bright colors and also in some color combinations. The blended colors and pastel shades sell well to French and English buyers, while Germans seem to prefer bright, bold colors.

The Vagaries of Fashion

Knowing where flowers will be sold is important to commercial hybridizers. At the major breeding centers for roses, mums, alstroemerias, and orchids, breeders must offer growers the sort of flowers that are in demand. Sometimes it is difficult to predict several years ahead, because fashions for colors and even flower species can change quickly. For a few years many designers may want white orchids for wedding work, then almost overnight white is out and pink is in!

Looks, Growth Habit, and Size

Hybridizers also select for flower placement, production, and size. At Van Staaveren I learned that their new Peruvian lilies *(Alstroemeria)* are bred for multiple open flowers on a two-tiered umbel. Older types have only one or two flowers open at a time. New hybrids have four to seven, plus secondary buds that often open as the first flowers fade.

Long-lasting flowers with full, overlapping petal shape are also goals of alstroemeria breeders. New colors in all flower types are an economic asset to breeders and hybridizers. Being able to offer something new to designers and consumers increases sales.

In addition to all these goals, plant growth habit is also important. Alstroemerias grow with a twining stem, making support necessary. Hybridizers try to increase stem strength while still breeding plants that stay compact and tend to bloom over a period of many months.

Bigger is not always better for cut flowers. The average retail buyer needs flowers of moderate size to be in proper scale for home arrangements. Medium to small flowers are often easier to pick and ship, so growers also appreciate that sometimes less is more. Designers may find it easier to work with flowers of moderate size. Plant breeders keep these factors in mind when developing new strains.

A recent example involves gerberas, one of the ten most popular flowers in the world. Some of the larger gerbera flowers have weak necks and blooms too large for some designs. With these drawbacks in mind, the Dutch firm Terra Nigra developed a new group of miniature gerberas which they called 'Germini' hybrids.

One of the world's most popular cut flowers, gerbera hybrids are on sale at the Los Angeles flower market.

'Germini' gerberas grow on compact plants. They are good commercial producers with a rapid second bloom, and they were bred to have strong necks that help flowers stay erect. These new gerberas are only two to three inches across, but their colors are as pure as those of their larger relatives. Thanks to modern tissue culture, Terra Nigra in Holland can now quickly propagate thousands of plants for worldwide sales to commercial growers.

Soon after the 'Germini' hybrids were introduced, managers of Maxima Farms, a firm based in Bogota, Colombia, purchased many plants. Now the new selections are available as imported fresh flowers, coming to the United States through the port of Miami. Similar stories can be told about new chrysanthemums, roses, lilies, and other popular cut flowers.

Who Buys the Most?

Commercial plant breeders and growers keep their eye on who buys plant products. Yearly the Flower Council of Holland surveys the purchasing trends of fresh flowers.

According to the Flower Council of Holland, Italy leads the world in per capita consumption of cut flowers. The table below lists the 1990 figures for several countries, giving the amount in U.S. dollars of money spent per person on fresh flowers. Figures are based on 1.885 Dutch guilders to $1.00 U.S.

Country	Amount	Country	Amount
Italy	$68.43	Denmark	$32.89
Norway	$60.47	Austria	$32.89
Switzerland	$57.29	Belgium	$32.36
Japan	$45.62	France	$26.52
West Germany	$45.09	United States	$22.81
Sweden	$42.97	United Kingdom	$20.15
Holland	$39.25	Spain	$10.61

Roses Are Red...and Many Other Colors!

The world's favorite flowers are roses, according to international surveys and figures from the major cut-flower auctions. The Society of American Florists reports that on a recent Valentine's Day, Americans bought about 75 million roses. The Flower Council of Holland reports over 2 billion roses sold through Dutch auctions in 1991. Gaining fast in popularity are the small flowered varieties, broadly labeled "Spray" roses by florists. This group includes many floribunda and slightly smaller flowered polyantha hybrids.

Red is the most popular color of rose, accounting for 80 percent of sales in the United States, followed by yellow, then pink. One of the most famous reds is the hybrid tea 'Royalty', appreciated for its light fragrance, elegantly shaped buds, and long vase life. Wright Brothers Roses in Utah, a major American rose grower, reports that 'Royalty' accounts for 50 to 60 percent of their rose sales.

Because roses are so popular as cut flowers and in the garden, they are a leading focus of plant breeders. Major rose hybridizers are continually introducing new creations, mainly from breeding farms in England, France, Germany, and the United States. The best hybrids are exchanged between hybridizers and growing firms on a royalty basis. For example, a rose, such as 'Perfect Moment', created by Reimer Kordes in Germany, is grown and sold by several firms in the United States, including Jackson and Perkins and the Conard-Pyle Company.

Similar arrangements are used for roses bred in the United States but grown and sold in other countries. Whether they are created for cut-flower growers or the garden, new rose hybrids go through the same strict steps of evaluation, quality control, and testing before being offered for sale as plants.

To get an idea of how a new rose is brought to market, consider the histories of two 1991 All-America Rose Selections. The AARS is a non-profit organization of U.S. rose producers designed to test new rose introductions. Over several seasons and in gardens throughout the

48

Rose 'Sheer Elegance' displays a typical Hybrid Tea form with many tightly packed wide petals opening from a graceful conical bud. The long-stemmed roses that are so popular as special gifts, are mainly Hybrid Tea types.

United States, new hybrids are scored for vigor, growth habit, disease resistance, flower production, color, form, fragrance, and other characteristics important in outstanding roses. 'Sheer Elegance' is a hybrid tea rose bred by Jerry Twomey and introduced by DeVor Nurseries of Watsonville, California. 'Shining Hour' is a grandiflora rose developed by William A. Warriner and introduced by Jackson and Perkins.

'SHEER ELEGANCE': BREEDING HISTORY
Summer 1981: Parents 'Pristine' and 'Fortuna' crossed for seed.
December 1981: Seed planted.

Spring 1982: First flowering of seedlings, best are chosen to grow for testing.

Spring 1983: Best candidates grafted for field testing.

Seasons 1983 to 1986: Field evaluations include checks for vigor, disease resistance, and flower quality.

Fall 1987: Hybrid, under code number, entered into AARS trials for testing in many regions.

1991: 'Sheer Elegance' selected as a winner by AARS judges and scheduled for release, spring 1991.

'SHINING HOUR': BREEDING HISTORY

June 1981: Hybridizer William A. Warriner crosses parents 'Sunbright' and 'Sunflare' to get seed.

December 1981: Seed sown.

March 1982: First seedlings bloom.

April to July 1982: Best seedlings are identified in the seedling beds and given code numbers.

July 1982: One of the best (later registered as 'Shining Hour') increased to 6 plants by bud grafting.

May 1984: Increased to 50 plants for more testing.

1986 season: Increased to 500 plants.

1987: Increased to 5,000 plants for extensive multizone tests in AARS trials.

1988 season: Gets high trial marks by official AARS judges; Jackson and Perkins propagates 20,000 plants.

1989 to 1990: More propagation for commercial release as AARS in spring 1991.

Breeding new roses for commercial introduction is costly. Jackson and Perkins reports: "A young seedling's merits are carefully evaluated for up to 10 years before the rose is introduced, at an investment of $75,000.00 to $100,000.00 for each rose that finally reaches the gardening public."

Rose 'Shining Hour' combines two desirable features: the abundant flowering of a Floribunda rose with the shape of a Hybrid Tea. This blend, referred to as a Grandiflora, produces flowers that are intermediate in size between Hybrid Teas and Floribundas. In contrast to pure Floribundas, Grandifloras have longer stems and flowers that are more formally shaped—characteristics inherited from Hybrid Teas.

At the Meilland rose fields in southern France newly bred roses (top) are rigorously tested for such characteristics as consistency and resistance to disease.

Hybridizers protect freshly pollinated parent flowers (above) from bees and rain with paper caps.

Garden or Greenhouse?

What is the difference between rose hybrids grown in the garden and those chosen as hybrids for cut flower production? Some important distinctions involve commercial considerations. Roses used for cut flowers must stand up to handling, packing, and shipping. They should have well-formed buds that do not open too quickly. Roses grown under glass or in warm climates for the cut-flower trade do not have to be cold hardy. Some beautiful hybrids are unsuitable for gardens in many parts of the world because they do not survive very cold winters.

To find out more about modern rose breeding trends I talked with Dr. Keith Zary, hybridizer and director of rose research at Jackson and Perkins Company. Dr. Zary supervises the largest rose-hybridizing program in the United States, involving more than 400,000 new seedlings each year. From this vast number of rose plants Dr. Zary and staff select only the best for future testing. From the very best individuals come the final introductions for both cut-flower roses and garden types.

Dr. Zary explained that by the 1920s, the breeding lines between garden roses and the cut-flower types had begun to diverge, separated on the basis of which roses flowered most successfully under glass during winter months. An excellent garden rose may produce beautiful long-lasting flowers under summer sun but only weak, flowerless stems when forced under glass in the winter. Commercial rose growers need hybrids that will bloom well with lower light intensities in winter, either outdoors in warm climates (in places such as Mexico, Colombia, and Ecuador) or under glass in cold climates.

To breed roses suitable for year-round production as cut flowers, hybridizers select parents that produce well with minimum light intensities. Sometimes a rose hybrid will be suitable both for winter production and garden use, but most roses found at florists' shops have been bred as cut-flower types. Similar routines are followed by rose breeders around the world. Many breed roses for garden and cut-flower use. When I visited the growing fields of Meilland in the south of

France, mainly to investigate their miniature rose breeding, I saw that their breeders stress rigorous field testing of new seedlings. Any weak plants are eliminated. Only disease-resistant plants with impressive flowers are saved for future evaluation.

'Carefree Wonder', a 1991 Selection Meilland introduction that was an All-America Rose Selection as an outstanding garden rose, also has flowers that are delightful in arrangements. As an everblooming garden rose with semidouble pink flowers, 'Carefree Wonder' manages to provide a season-long supply of cottage-style flowers, perfect for relaxed country bouquets.

Miniature Roses

As a gardener who enjoys raising flowers for arrangements, I find many of the miniature roses—only just starting to be popular as a cut flower—bloom well in the winter when grown under wide-spectrum fluorescent light or at a sunny window. The same hybrids are sturdy cold-hardy garden plants that blossom from spring into fall outdoors.

Propagation of Roses

Larger garden roses and cut-flower hybrids are propagated by grafting a bud of the hybrid onto a rootstock of a common sturdy rose, such as *Rosa multiflora* (a wild, or species, rose) or 'Dr. Huey', an old climber hybrid. Except when used to make rose trees on a tall stem, miniature roses are vegetatively propagated from stem cuttings, not grafted onto different rootstocks. Field budding of cut-flower roses is done on the vigorous but less cold-hardy *Rosa x noisettiana manettii*, or the old tea rose, *Rosa x odorata*, which roots quickly under the mist in the propagator's grafting range.

Surprise Mutations

Not all new roses originate as hybrids. Some popular roses, including many grown as cut-flower crops, were surprise mutations, or sports. When growers discover a plant of a standard hybrid that produces flowers of a different color, they isolate the bush. After watching the mutated plant

Among the well-known new hybrids developed at the rose breeding firm of Meilland is 'Carefree Wonder', a 1991 All-America Rose Selection, shown on page 96.

for several flowerings, to be sure the change is stable, a grower may choose to introduce the new mutation with its own hybrid names.

Examples of cut-flower roses that were discovered as mutations include dark red 'Idole', a sport of the orange-red 'Madelon'; 'Bridal White', from 'Bridal Pink'; and the soft pink 'Darling' from the well-known, salmon-colored 'Sonia'.

Chrysanthemums

Second in world popularity are chrysanthemums. They owe this position mainly to the hybridizers, who have created many outstanding introductions, and to the growers, who produce sturdy cut mums with long vase life.

Efficient modern flower farms combine advanced computer technology, precise agricultural science, and an extraordinary amount of hand labor. Toucan Flowers, chrysanthemum specialists in Costa Rica, is a good example of such a farm.

On one of my research visits I learned that Toucan Flowers sells 80 percent of its chrysanthemum crop to Condor Farms, a Miami-based wholesale importer/distributor. From the Miami cooling rooms, thousands of cut mums are distributed throughout the United States. Some of the imports are used by Sterling Bouquet, a sister firm that makes arrangements for major supermarkets.

Once a new mum variety is developed, test plants are sent to major growers in several countries. The growers evaluate field performance and sometimes send sample cuts to wholesalers for further evaluation. Finally, as at Toucan Flowers, the plants chosen are mass-propagated for future flower production.

Every week Toucan Flowers workers root a million chrysanthemum cuttings to furnish plants for cut flowers. The process begins with a small number of unrooted tip cuttings of new hybrids, which are rushed to Toucan from such major hybridizers as Yoder Brothers in the United States and Fides in Holland. These master cuttings are rooted under mist in 10 to 12 days, and the new hybrid plants are cultivated as mother clumps, each designed to furnish more cuttings. The secondary tip cuttings produced at Toucan growing ranges will be the plants that finally produce the beautiful mums we enjoy.

Toucan grows about 100 different mum hybrids, more than half of which are cultivated for the U.S. market. Boxes of flowers, each containing 20 or 40 mixed-color bunches, are sent to wholesalers in cargo planes every night. Colors in each box are coordinated according to market performances, often tailored to major holidays (with white predominating at Christmas, the warmer bronze and yellow for Thanksgiving, and yellow and white for Easter).

With such precise demands a modern flower farm must time plantings, crop types, and harvesting exactly. At Toucan, the workers root about a million cuttings per week, of which around 600,000 of the strongest are planted out for flowering.

Chrysanthemums initiate flower buds when nights are long. To keep plants in a vegetative (nonflowering) mode until the timing on the market is right, some growers extend the "day"—by providing artificial lights at night. When the time is right for the mums to go to market, the night lights are switched off.

Once night lights are canceled, the mum plants make flower buds and bloom in about 12 weeks. By timing plantings and light cycles growers bring flowers to market with precision.

Flowers whose blooms cannot be timed in this way—such as roses and carnations—may be stored in big coolers at just above freezing until peak market demand.

Orchids and Tropicals

Growers of tropical flowers usually specialize in compatible crops. Anthuriums, gingers, and tropical foliage, for example, are sold by scores of firms in Hawaii. In contrast, the major orchid growers are specialists; the orchid firms I visited in California, Florida, Indonesia, Malaysia,

Above. In the growing ranges harvested mums are kept in protective sleeves with their stems in water in preparation for export.

Opposite. At Toucan Flowers mother clumps of chrysanthemums (top) supply one million cuttings per week. These fresh tips root in 10 to12 days under mist (second from top). The cuttings are put in color-coded trays (second from bottom) that are used to sort different hybrids. Cuttings produce flowering plants after several months growth (bottom).

Page 56. Orchids are an important export for several Asian countries. In Bangkok a co-op flower center (top) handles flowers from many growers, including these famous Thai dendrobiums. At Flora Alam in Java (center), Indonesian hybrid dendrobiums need the protection of shade cloths. At Kun Somksat's growing range near Bangkok, (bottom) 100,000 dendrobiums, among them this hybrid Dendrobium Sonia, seen here in bloom, produce flowers all year long.

Pages 56 and 57.
Vanda hybrids, mainly *Mokara* Chark Kuan, grow outdoors at the Chong nursery in Seramban, Malaysia.

Mokara orchids, complex hybrids of *Vanda,* with related genera thrive in outdoor beds in Malaysia.

Singapore, and Thailand export orchids exclusively. Most firms offer a mix of genera, mainly improved modern hybrids propagated from superior clones by tissue culture.

Genera such as *Dendrobium, Cattleya, Cymbidium,* and *Vanda* hybrids are so popular as cut flowers that thousands of select clones are propagated on nutrient agar (a gelatinous alga extract used as a propagation medium by tissue-culture labs. Some growers propagate their own plants but others rely on purchasing propagations from specialized tissue-culture labs.

Hybridizers make crosses between two superior parents, then sow thousands of seeds on nutrient agar in sterile flasks. After two to ten years—depending on the genus and parent—the seedlings begin to flower. From the thousands of first-bloom seedlings, only a few truly superior individuals (clones) will be kept for further evaluation.

A small mass of tissue is cut from the growing point, or meristem, of selected hybrids. This tissue is grown on nutrient agar, much like the original seeds, but these clones will be genetically identical to the original tissue donor. In a few years a grower can have thousands of identically superior orchids producing flowers for cutting.

Orchids are propagated sexually from seed or asexually from meristem tissues. Both methods rely on nutrient agar inside sterile flasks to nourish the plantlets.

Color Favorites

Professional orchid hybridizers are aware of cultural color preferences. One such individual is George Vasquez of Zuma Canyon Orchids in Malibu, California, who travels around the world to sell his unique *Phalaenopsis* hybrids. In a recent American Orchid Society Bulletin he describes his earlier trips to Asia where he was unaware of national color preferences (George Vasquez with Mary Carol Frier "International Tastes in Phalaenopsis Hybrids," *American Orchid Society Bulletin* 60 [January 1991]).

"I brought red and yellow *Phalaenopsis* to Japan and could not sell them. When I traveled to Taiwan I took only whites . . . I picked the wrong color again; people (in Taiwan) didn't want whites. Instead the reds and yellows were in tremendous demand."

This hybrid *Phalaenopsis* of *P. Leilehua,* with species *P. violacea,* was bred by Michael Ooi in Penang, Malaysia. The leathery flowers last many weeks on the plant.

Mr. Vasquez explains that although the taste in white *Phalaenopsis* is not static, the older population base of Japan grew up appreciating flowers of pure white or pure pink, rather than mixed or spotted colors. Around the world, Mr. Vasquez reports, younger consumers are leaning toward brighter hues in yellows, pinks, and smooth pastel colors.

Michael Ooi, a species *Phalaenopsis* specialist in Malaysia, works to incorporate the waxy substance and fragrance of small-flowered Malaysian species into larger hybrids. Some of his crosses using *Phalaenopsis violacea* (a small-flowered species) with large standard whites produced heavy, slightly waxy large flowers with an attractive pink center blush from the species parent.

I grow many of the Zuma Canyon striped *Phalaenopsis* in my own collection of orchids, and I find them to be long-lasting cut flowers adaptable to many styles of design. When visiting wholesale markets and florists I often see the classic arching sprays of white *Phalaenopsis* hybrids, but they are increasingly joined by more brightly colored hybrids, sometimes even 1- or 2-inch waxy orange or yellow hybrids. *Phalaenopsis* are a good buy in orchids. They last a week or more in water, often more than a month on the plant. A cut spray need not be used whole; individual flowers have long enough stems to be used with water tubes or in shallow dishes. Their flat shape makes *Phalaenopsis* ideal as a corsage flower or to decorate gifts.

Gross Propagation

Certain specialty crops can be propagated quickly by gross division of parent plants. This asexual system produces offspring identical to the parent. Heliconias are a good example of a popular specialty flower that is marketed through mass propagation. All over the tropical world I have admired heliconias in landscape designs; in jungles of the New World they grow under humid, warm conditions. I visited Costa Flores in Costa Rica to study how heliconias are grown for the cut-flower trade.

David Carli, the owner of Costa Flores, has collected superior heliconias in many jungle habitats. He reports that an average heliconia clump can be divided into 30 to 100 growing plants, sometimes called "eyes." Even a plant grown from seed usually develops many growing points by the time it blooms, two to three years after sowing.

At the plantation of Costa Flores in Costa Rica, heliconias are harvested from humid tropical fields (top) then washed and polished before being exported. A custom order sheet (above) codes each stalk to the final buyer.

61

In less than a year, under favorable tropical conditions, each heliconia division will yield 30 to 100 more plants. With such a prolific production of natural offsets, the commercial grower can have a plantation of superior clones in two years. To maintain maximum productivity, established clumps of most showy heliconias must be divided every two to three years.

The gingers and ornamental bananas, two other tropicals, are easier to grow since they bloom well many years without being divided. The ornamental bananas, calatheas, and various flowering gingers are good companion crops since they require similar warm humid conditions. Both heliconias and these companion plants are labor-intensive as cut flowers. At Costa Flores they are cultivated on four farms carved out of the Atlantic slope jungle, a warm rainy habitat where some of the species grow naturally.

Disease and insect pests are controlled with regular preventive spraying and crop rotation. Interspersing genera and isolating growing beds with deep drainage ditches also helps keep tropical flower crops healthy.

Transporting Fresh Tropicals

Growing and shipping large, fragile, heavy tropicals such as heliconias and gingers is costly. About 25 percent of the flower's final price covers growing, picking, cleaning, and packing; another 25 percent is added for shipping. Thus profits for the grower, importer, wholesaler, and retail florist all must be derived from the remaining 50 percent of the selling price.

To minimize loss, Costa Flores sells in advance all the flowers they cut. A network of faxes and computers connects the growing range with the Miami-based marketing office of Floral Resources Hawaii, a wholesale distributor of Costa Flores crops. Each week field managers in Costa Rica walk through their plantations to estimate a possible harvest from more than 200 different flowering tropical plants. These extensive plantation observations are necessary because the crops are so diverse in seasonal differences and stages of growth. Mature heliconias produce an average of one flowering stalk per week, but some species only bloom a few weeks each year, others on and off all year long.

The estimated harvest figures are faxed to Miami, where marketing personnel call major customers, mainly wholesalers. Orders gathered in this fashion are faxed to Costa Rica where the flowers are cut, according to specific lists carried into the growing beds by supervisors.

A Trolley Ride

The trip from the jungle growing beds to the customer begins with a trolley ride. David Carli borrowed technology from banana growers when he built an extensive overhead trolley system through his jungle growing fields. His company purchased some of the metal posts and related equipment from Central American banana plantation owners. To accommodate the long stalks of heliconias, gingers, and the flowering bananas, David Carli replaced the big hooks used in banana plantations with specially designed plastic tubes and metal cylinders.

Thanks to this inventive application of agricultural technology, the Costa Flores workers can quickly harvest hundreds of stalks holding delicate flowers in a very short time. I watched workers almost rush through rows of 15- to 20-foot heliconia plants, slashing stalks with one swipe of a sharp machete, carefully carrying cut stems through muddy growing fields to the overhead trolley line, and setting them individually into holding tubes. From here, the flowers take a hand-assisted trolley ride to a central gathering point. Once enough stalks have been cut they are loaded off the monorail into massed cylinders for truck transport to a cleaning and packing building. At Costa Flores Friday is the day of major harvesting, and the flowers have the weekend to travel by air to Miami.

Complex flowers like heliconias are dipped in pesticide, hand washed and dried, and sometimes shined with mineral oil—then packed.

Top. An overhead trolley transports freshly cut heliconia stems at Costa Flores.

Above. Ti leaves that have been washed await shipping from a jungle depot. Bright crotons thrive in a field beyond.

Opposite. Rare clones of *Cordyline terminalis* (top) flourish under a shade cloth at Costa Flores. In a packing shed (bottom) red ginger and *Cordyline terminalis* leaves are kept fresh under mist until they are packed for export.

63

To make this exotic arrangement from materials in a Costa Flores tropical design kit, use a heavy kenzan dish that has a pin holder inside a water dish. The flowers and foliage include *Calathea crotolifera*, croton leaf, *Sansevieria trifasciata*, *Cordyline terminalis* 'Compacta Royale', and stems of *Tapeinochilos ananassae*.

Agricultural inspection at Miami is strict, so each shipment must be free from harmful pests. After cleaning and drip drying the flowering stalks are packed for shipping. Some of the gingers, such as *Alpinia,* are kept under mist until just before packing.

Besides the exotic heliconias and gingers, Costa Flores grows a broad assortment of beautiful foliage plants. David Carli has extensive beds under plastic shade cloth where unusual new clones of calathea, cordyline, and croton are evaluated. Costa Flores uses the tropical foliage and bold flowers to make intriguing boxed assortments of varying sizes, each featuring one major flowering stalk and complementary foliage. Inside each sturdy box is a folder giving arrangement suggestions, care points, and some romantic text about the origins of tropical flowers. A small bottle of "Jungle Juice" (scented mineral oil) is included as a polish and antitranspirant rub for shiny heliconias and some of the glossy leaves such as crotons. I like these self-contained tropical designer arrangements because the flowers are fresh, well packed, and offer an assortment not easily duplicated except by visiting a well-stocked wholesale specialist.

Gardenias and Other Specialty Flowers

Lesser-known specialty flowers are grown by smaller farms or as sidelines at farms featuring major favorites. A chrysanthemum grower, for example, may sell some statice or assorted cut foliage. Rod McLellan Company, an orchid supplier in south San Francisco, also grows gardenias, stephanotises, eucalyptus foliage, and some cut-flower roses. McLellan first introduced "tailored" gardenias in 1937. Now the company's premium-quality corsages are shipped to florists all over the United States.

These tailored gardenias begin as half-open buds, picked each morning from gardenia shrubs in the greenhouse growing range. The blooms rest on moist paper in a humid walk-in cooler until needed by the groomer. Using a very gentle touch (since gardenias show brown stains if pinched), a groomer carefully opens the outer petals; with the lower

Gardenia corsages fashioned at the
Rod McLellan Company in San
Francisco begin with freshly picked,
partially open buds (top left) that
are formed by hand into open
corsages (top right) and inserted
into a quartet of freshly washed
leaves (above). The well-groomed,
fragrant corsages are packed in
protective boxes (right) for delivery
to florists.

petals bent down, only a tight center cluster remains upright, forming the beautiful and familiar corsage flower.

The best flowers are inserted into a collar formed by four gardenia leaves stapled to a round cardboard support. Smaller or less perfect tailored gardenias are given a collar of plastic leaves. Completed corsages are packed in protective cardboard boxes with see-through lids, all covered in moisture-retaining wrap. Gardenias absorb little water through the stem once cut so high humidity is important for maximum corsage life. Optimum storage temperature is just above freezing to around 40° F.

Gardenia corsages are relatively expensive because of the hand labor involved and the short storage life once cut. And although gardenia shrubs live for decades, commercial growers replace them after four or five years to maintain bush vigor. February through June is peak demand time for gardenia corsages, but plants in greenhouses can bloom anytime, if temperature and light are manipulated properly.

Stephanotises, clustered white flowers with a heavy perfume similar to that of gardenias, are grown and stored like gardenias but the flowers are produced on vines. You will often find gardenias and stephanotises next to each other in florists' coolers. Both of these fragrant white flowers can be kept without water for several days as long as they are cool and in an area within 90 to 100 percent humidity.

Some growers devote themselves to lesser-known fresh flowers, often grown from seed as annuals or biennials. The Association of Specialty Cut Flower Growers is a group dedicated to helping growers of unusual flowers. The growers in turn work to improve flower selection, quality, and consumer acceptance. Yearly field trials and ongoing research at various universities help educate growers about new selections and optimum growing methods.

Anthuriums and Various Hawaiian Delights

Most anthuriums sold in the United States are grown in Hawaii by more than 80 commercial growers. An anthurium growers cooperative based in

Hilo helps market many of these nationally grown flowers. Other exotic imports commercially cultivated in Hawaii include Asian gingers, orchids, heliconia species from Latin America, and numerous types of tropical foliage, from alocasia to zingiber.

A few Hawaiian growers will sell and ship retail orders, but most sell through wholesalers. Thousands of Hawaiian flowers are used daily just a few miles from where they are grown. Hawaiian hotels, resorts, and restaurants often hire professional designers on a regular basis. Sometimes designers are full-time staff members, employed just to create a constant parade of tropical arrangements. Visitors find an opportunity to learn about hundreds of different tropical flowers in the Hawaiian Islands.

Flowering Bulbs

Some of the most beautiful cut flowers grow from underground corms, tubers, rhizomes, and roots, all popularly called bulbs. Tropical examples are the striking callas *(Zantedeschia)* and amaryllis. Better known are the many spring and summer flowering bulbs such as daffodils *(Narcissus* hybrids), freesias, hyacinths, lilies, and tulips. A host of small bulbs bring color to the early spring garden. Later underground corms produce gladiolus and crocosmias.

The Netherlands is the world's most famous bulb-growing nation. For more than 400 years the Dutch have cultivated and sold bulbs; in 1990, the Dutch bulb harvest was approximately 10 billion bulbs. About 10 percent—a billion—were sold to gardeners and commercial growers in the United States.

California growers produce many of the colorful calla lilies seen in the flower trade. Glads and daffodils are also commercial cut flower crops in several states. In the spring, garden centers and supermarkets feature pots of blooming miniature daffodils, often the small fragrant hybrid 'Tête à Tête'. You can join the fun by growing paperwhite narcissus and amaryllis *(Hippeastrum)* at home in the winter or glads, lilies, and other summer bulbs outdoors.

Pages 68 and 69.
In California's Lompoc valley, the Denholm Seed Company cultivates acres of hybrids, including such popular cut flowers as these glorious stock.

67

Hybrid 'Apollo' marigolds are bred at the Bodger Seed Company in California by alternating blocks of a male parent (orange) and a female parent, here a much less showy yellow.

Seed-Grown Crops

Fresh flower crops grown from seed can be planted faster than other types, and they require growers to invest less money per plant. The selection of cultivars is important, however. Plant breeders work just as hard on crops sold as seed as on plants offered as tissue-culture plantlets, grafts, and divisions.

Uniformity is important to growers of cut flowers. If a grower sows seed for white flowers, the resulting plants must produce almost 100 percent white flowers, not a mixture of colors. Before a crop is sown, the grower should know flower size, stem length, season of bloom, and other such characteristics; but such factors can be difficult to determine for seed-grown flowers. Consequently, seed-producing firms take years to develop predictable plants.

Many modern seed-grown flowers are controlled hybrids, grown using hand-pollination, isolation, and other methods to regulate pollination. The seed is collected from plants that have been pollinated with known male plants. This practice offers seed producers much more mastery over the resulting plants than with seedlings grown from open-pollinated plants.

Many costly hybrids, such as modern geraniums, petunias, and impatiens, are produced by hand-pollinating female plants in a greenhouse. Each flower is emasculated so it will not set seed with its own pollen. Then pollen from a desired male is dusted onto the stigmas of the female parent. A similar system may be used with snapdragons and other crops grown outdoors; growers often then place a mesh bag or other barrier over the pollinated flowers to keep out bees, which might mix unwanted pollen with the hand-placed grains.

There are some drawbacks to growing plants from seed. Some unusual cultivars are only available as asexual propagations. Moreover, with plantlets or divisions there is less chance of variations than with seed. Some crops can be produced a year or more faster from plantlets or divisions than if grown from seed. Bulbs, for example, may need three or

four years of growing before producing a flower. Cut-flower farmers wanting to sell daffodils or callas are naturally most likely to buy bulbs.

On the other hand, seed is often a less costly way to grow many plants, even when the extra time and labor are considered. Seed-grown plants are unlikely to have virus problems, and seed is easy to ship. Dry seed requires less strict agricultural inspection and is not as costly to transport. Finally, seed is easy to store until the grower wants to sow.

Some companies help cut-flower growers by sowing seed and then selling very small, sturdy seedlings, called plugs. Plugs involve less labor in sowing than do seeds, and they afford an opportunity to order a precise number of seedlings without any germination worries.

Potted Flowering Plants

Strict agricultural inspection rules make it difficult to import potted plants from other areas into the United States. Nonetheless, there is a fairly

In Gilroy, California, the Goldsmith Seed Company produces hybrid seed of many popular flowers, among them the snapdragons shown here. In growing trials new creations are tested to determine the improved types for future production and for commercial release.

brisk market in houseplants. According to the United States Department of Agriculture, potted flowering plants gained $522 million in wholesale sales in 1989. Poinsettias were the top earners, followed by chrysanthemums, azaleas, Easter lilies, and African violets. About 50 percent of all blooming potted plants are grown in only six states, led by California.

Both as cut stems and on potted plants, poinsettias last an impressively long time. The Paul Ecke Poinsettia Ranch in Encinitas, California, offers more than 80 different sizes, shapes, and colors of poinsettias. Growers in many countries start their poinsettia plants from cuttings raised at the Ecke Ranch, where poinsettias have been bred since the 1920s. I enjoy potted poinsettias from mid-December into April, sometimes cutting a few stems to mix with fresh flowers in arrangements. Paul Ecke, Jr., told me that most consumers, however, want poinsettias as Christmas flowers but not at other times of the year.

Fortunately, azaleas and chrysanthemums sell well both around and between major holidays. Small potted azaleas and miniature cyclamen are excellent focal points for table arrangements combining cut flowers with potted plants. Visit a local greenhouse, florist, or supermarket to select potted flowering plants. Be sure to ask for printed care notes to help you understand the culture of each plant.

With basic attention many flowering plants will last for months. Many popular azaleas and chrysanthemums sold in winter bloom, however, are bred for greenhouse growing. These types will not live outside through very cold winters but will do well in cool, sunny rooms where winter nights reach 40° to 50° F. Other favorite potted flowering plants such as spring daffodils, hyacinths, tulips, and many lilies are fully cold hardy. If you have some outdoor space, plant the bulbs outside in the late spring. Most will survive to bloom many years as garden plants.

Opposite.
Potted poinsettias available during the Christmas season will last for months when given proper care.

4.
IDENTIFICATION GUIDE TO POPULAR FRESH FLOWERS

To help you identify the most popular cut flowers and make quick selections for decoration and arrangements, I have grouped the flowers in this section visually according to broad types. Some groupings are based on specific related groups, such as orchids and roses. Other flowers are grouped according to their general shape and structure, such as daisy types or clusters. Within each grouping, flowers are arranged by look-alikes. An alphabetical listing for each group precedes each of the seven photo galleries of flowers.

In this chapter I have tried to help you with the decorative use of fresh flowers. All of the flower names are horticulturally correct, although my grouping criteria are visual rather than strictly botanical. I have listed each flower by its most common name—either the English or Latin name.

Each picture caption gives the name of the flower selected to typify its relatives as well as a page reference to the chart section where you will find basic information listed by the flower's genus.

Getting Acquainted

If you are a newcomer to the pleasures of flower arranging, you may wish

Bird of Paradise *(Strelitzia reginae)*, p. 247

to start with some of the most popular types: roses, chrysanthemums, carnations, tulips, lilies, freesias, gerberas, baby's breath, cymbidiums, or alstroemerias. All of these kinds are readily available from florists and supermarkets in the United States.

These flowers will give you a start, but I recommend that you become acquainted with rarer flowers as well. Some of the tropical exotics and locally grown garden flowers are exciting plants for unusual home arrangements.

Following are the broad groupings of flower types, showing popular flowers in each category, by common names. The chart in the appendices is in alphabetical order, by correct botanical genus name, a system that will help you communicate in the precise language of science.

I. DAISY TYPES: SINGLE AND DOUBLE, ROUND FLOWERS

Anemone	*Dahlia*
Anthemis	*Gardenia*
Aster	*Gerbera*
Astrantia	*Hibiscus*
Black-eyed Susan (*Rudbeckia*)	Marigold (*Tagetes*)
Calendula	Peony
Camellia	Poppy (*Papaver*)
Carnation (*Dianthus*)	*Ranunculus*
Christmas rose (*Helleborus*)	*Scabiosa*
Chrysanthemum	Sunflower (*Helianthus*)
Clarkia (*Godetia*)	Tansy (*Tanacetum vulgare*)
Clematis	*Trachelium*
Coreopsis	*Zinnia*
Cosmos	

Gardenia, p. 234

Left.
Tree peony 'Jitsugetsu Nishiki', p. 242

Page 80. Top row, left to right: Tree peonies 'Godaishu' (left), 'Higurashi' (top), and 'Ayagoromo' (right), p. 242; *Zinnia* 'Zenith', p. 249; *Clematis* 'Piccadilly', p. 227.
Bottom row, left to right: *Scabiosa caucasia* hybrid, p. 245; Cactus type *Dahlia* 'Alfred Grill', p. 230; Marigold 'Happy Days' (*Tagetes* hybrid), p. 247.

Page 81. *Gerbera* 'Silvia', p. 234

Above. *Cosmos bipinnatus* hybrid, p. 228

Opposite.
Top row, left to right: China asters *(Callistephus chinensis)*, p. 226;
Chrysanthemum 'Adorn', p. 227; *Astrantia major*, p. 225.
Bottom row, left to right: Camellia 'Debutante', p. 226; *Godetia grandiflora*, p. 235; Marigold 'Happy Red' *(Tagetes* hybrid),
p. 247.

Oriental poppy hybrid *(Papaver orientale)*, p. 242

Christmas rose *(Helleborus orientalis)*, p. 236

Page 86.
Top row, left to right: *Ranunculus* hybrids, p. 244; *Coreopsis* 'Early Sunrise', p. 228; Tansy *(Tanacetum vulgare)*, p. 247.
Bottom row, left to right: Black-eyed Susan Gloriosa hybrids *(Rudbeckia)*, p. 245; *Calendula* 'Pacific Beauty', p. 225; Hibiscus 'Lemon Chiffon' (*Hibiscus rosa-sinensis* hybrid), p. 237.

Page 87. Sunflower *(Helianthus annuus)*, p. 236

2. LILY-LIKE: SIMPLE, BOLD, ONE-COLOR OR MULTICOLORED

Agapanthus

Amaryllis

Anthurium

Calla *(Zantedeschia)*

Daylily *(Hemerocallis)*

Eucharis lily *(Eucharis)*

Glory lily *(Gloriosa rothschildiana)*

Lily *(Lilium),* including Easter lily *(L. longiflorum), L. auratum*
    Oriental hybrids such as 'Casa Blanca' and 'Star Gazer' and colored types called Asian hybrids including 'Enchantment' and 'Yellow Giant'

Nerine

Peruvian lily *(Alstroemeria)*

Spathiphyllum

Right. Oriental lily 'Strawberry Shortcake' *(Lilium* hybrid), p. 239

Opposite. Eucharis lily *(Eucharis amazonica)*, p. 232

Page 90. Glory lily *(Gloriosa rothschildiana)*, p. 235

Page 91. Left row, top to bottom: *Agapanthus* 'Loch Hope', p. 221; *Nerine bowdenii*, p. 241; Peruvian lily *(Alstroemeria* 'Barbara'), p. 222; Right. *Nerine* 'Theresa Buxton', p. 241.

88

Top left. 'Casa Blanca' *(Lilium* hybrid), p. 239
Top right. Glory lily *(Gloriosa rothschildiana)* and curly hazel branch, p. 235
Bottom. Daylily *(Hemerocallis* hybrid). p. 236

Opposite. Lily 'Black Beauty', p. 239

Clockwise from top left.
Spathiphyllum 'Lynise', p. 246;
Anthurium Obaki hybrids, p. 223;
Calla lily 'Flame' *(Zantedeschia* hybrid),
p. 249;
Anthurium scherzerianum hybrid with
double spathe, p. 223.

Opposite. *Amaryllis* 'Minerva', p. 222

3. ROSES
Hybrid teas (standard large-flowered long-stemmed roses)
Miniature roses
Shrub roses (clusters of flowers such as 'Carefree Wonder', 'Bonica', and
  Mediland hybrids)
Spray roses (mainly hybrid floribundas and polyanthas)

Right. 'Carefree Wonder' shrub rose

Opposite.
Top left: 'Alba Mediland' shrub rose;
Bottom left: 'Bonica' shrub rose
Right: 'Grisbi' Sweetheart spray.

See p. 245

'Sonia' hybrid grandiflora tea

See p. 245

Left. Princess of Monaco' hybrid tea

Page 100. 'Kalinka' hybrid tea

Page 101. 'Chicago Peace' hybrid tea

See p. 245

Right. 'Scarlet Gem', 'Mimi', 'White Gem', 'Crimson Gem' miniatures

Opposite top. 'Arianna' and 'Supra' intermediate size hybrid teas with *Dizygotheca* leaves in Chinese teapot of the Qianlong period (1736-95) Opposite bottom. Bouquet of miniature rose hybrids

See p. 245

Below. Darwin hybrid tulip
'Gudoshnik', p. 248

Opposite. Tulip 'Merry Widow',
p. 248

4. SPRING BULB TYPES

Allium
Blue bells *(Scilla)*
Crocus
Cyclamen
Daffodil *(Narcissus)*
Freesia
Hyacinthus
Iris, Dutch, Spanish

Lily of the valley *(Convallaria majalis)*
Montbretia *(Crocosmia)*
Muscari
Ornithogalum
Triteleia
Tuberose *(Polianthes)*
Tulip

Far left. Montbretias 'Emily McKenzie' and 'James Coey' *(Crocosmia* hybrids), p. 228
Left. *Crocus corsicus,* p. 229
Below. Daffodils *(Narcissus* hybrids), p. 240

Opposite.
Left: Freesia hybrids, p. 234;
Top right: Tuberose *(Polianthes tuberosa),* p. 244;
Bottom right: *Cyclamen persicum* hybrid), p. 229.

Opposite.
Top left: Narcissus paperwhite hybrids, p. 240
Top right: Lily of the Valley (*Convallaria majalis* cultivars), p. 227
Bottom: *Ornithogalum thyrsoides* (left) and *O. arabicum* (right), p. 242

Left. Iris 'White Wedgewood', p. 237

Triteleia 'Queen Fabiola', p. 248

Muscari comosum, p. 240

Blue bells *(Scilla siberica)*, p. 246

Muscari 'Blue Spike', p. 240

Right.
Hyacinthus 'Amsterdam', p. 237

Opposite.
Allium 'Purple Sensation', p. 221

5. CLUSTERS AND MULTIFLOWERED STEMS

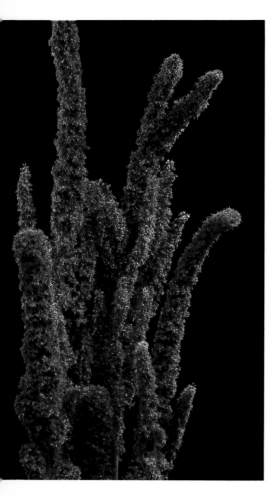

Amaranthus 'Pygmy Torch', p. 222

Amaranth
Astilbe
Baby's Breath (*Gypsophila*)
Balloon flower (*Platycodon*)
Bells of Ireland (*Moluccella*)
Bouvardia
Broom (*Cytisus*)
Celosia
Clerodendrum
Columbine (*Aquilegia*)
Delphinium
Dill (*Anethum*)
Echinops
Euphorbia fulgens, Poinsettia
    (*E. pulcherrima*)
Eustoma grandiflorum hybrids
    (syn. *Lisianthus*)
Fennel (*Foeniculum*)
Foxglove (*Digitalis*)
Foxtail lily (*Eremurus*)
Gladiolus
Goldenrod (*Solidago* and *Solidaster*)
Gomphrena
Heather (*Erica*)
Ixora

Kniphofia
Larkspur (*Consolida*, syn. *Delphinium ajacis*)
Lavender (*Lavandula*)
Liatris
Loosestrife (*Lysimachia*)
Mallow (*Lavatera*)
Mimosa (*Acacia*)
Mullen (*Verbascum*)
Nigella
Oregano (*Origanum*)
Phlox
Physostegia
Queen Anne's lace (cultivated *Ammi*,
    wild *Daucus*)
Salvia
Sea holly (*Eryngium*)
Sedum spectabile
Snapdragon (*Antirrhinum*)
Statice (*Limonium*)
Stephanotis
Stock (*Matthiola incana*)
Sweet pea (*Lathyrus*)
Trachelium caeruleum
Veronica
Yarrow (*Achillea*)

Celosia argentea var. *plumosa*, p. 226,
and green Bells of Ireland (*Moluccella*),
p. 240

Left. *Celosia* 'Pink Castle', p. 226

Opposite.
Left row, top to bottom:
Trachelium caeruleum, p. 248;
Astilbe 'Peach Blossom', p. 224;
Oregano *(Origanum vulgare)*,
p. 241.
Right row, top to bottom:
Baby's Breath *(Gypsophila paniculata*
'Rosy Veil')*, p. 235; Broom
(Cytisus canariensis tinted pink)*,
p. 229; *Bouvardia* 'Bridesmaid',
p. 225.

Top left. Larkspur (*Consolida* hybrids), p. 227
Top right. Foxglove (*Digitalis thapsi*), p. 231
Bottom left: Mallow (*Lavatera trimestris* hybrid). p. 238
Bottom right. Balloon flower (*Platycodon* hybrid), p. 244

Opposite, top and bottom: *Eustoma grandiflorum* hybrids, p. 233

Opposite.
Top row, left to right:
Golden Rod *(Solidago)*, p. 246; Mimosa *(Acacia baileyana)*, p. 221; Fennel *(Foeniculum vulgare* bronze type), p. 233.
Bottom row: Dill *(Anethum graveolens)*, p. 223; *Nigella damascena*, p. 241.

Top. Heather *Erica* 'Winter Beauty', p. 232
Center. Loosestrife *(Lysimachia clethroides)*, p. 239
Bottom. Queen Anne's Lace *(Ammi majus)*, pp. 222, 230

Page 122. Top: *Phlox* 'Bright Eyes', p. 243
Bottom: Sea Holly *(Eryngium)*, p. 232

Page 123. Top: Sweet pea *(Lathyrus odoratus* 'Super Snoop'), p, 238
Bottom: *Clerodendrum thomsoniae*, p. 227

Right. Gladiolus 'Traderhorn' and *Aucuba japonica* leaves, p. 234

Opposite.
Top row from left to right:
Kniphofia macowanii, p. 237; *Veronica* 'Sunny Border Blue', p. 249; *Physostegia virginiana variegata*, p. 243.

Bottom row, left to right:
Mullein *(Verbascum olympicum)* p. 248; *Liatris spicata*, p. 239; *Salvia* 'Sizzler Lavender', p. 245.

Snapdragon (*Antirrhinum* 'Bright
Butterflys'), p. 224

Yarrow (*Achillea* 'Coronation Gold'),
p. 221

Right. *Gomphrena globosa*, p. 235

Opposite.
Left. *Eremurus stenophyllus*, p. 232
Right. *Lavandula × intermedia*
'Grosso', p. 238

133

6. ORCHIDS: MANY GENERA, SPECIES, AND HYBRIDS

Cattleya
Cymbidium
Dendrobium (many Asian and Hawaiian hybrids)
Epidendrum
Lady's slipper (*Paphiopedilum* hybrids)
Odontoglossum
Oncidium (yellow spray orchids)
Phalaenopsis
Vanda (including *Vanda* hybrids like
    Aranthera, Ascocenda, Mokara)

1 *Cattleya* hybrids
2 *Phalaeopsis* hybrids
3 *Ascocentrum* and *Vanda* compact
  hybrids
4 *Epidendrum* hybrid
5 *Brassavola nodosa* "Lady of the
  Night" orchid
6 *Pleurothallis grobyi,* mini species
  from Amazon region
7 *Aspasia* hybrid

138

Page 136.
Laeliocattleya Adelade Waltman,
p. 226

Page 137.
Left row, top to bottom: *Cattleya*
Wavariana 'Talisman Cove';
Potinara Lemon Tree 'Yellow
Magic'; *Cattleya percivaliana*
'Summit'

Right row, top to bottom:
Laeliocattleya Fran Ascher and
Brassolaeliocattleya Memoria Crispin
Rosales; *Cattleya* Small World;
Cattleya Blue Bonnet

See p. 226

Left.
Cymbidium Mary Pinchess 'Del
Rey' with *Polyscia
guilfoylei* 'Victoriae', p. 229

Cymbidium Red Imp 'Red Tower', p. 229

Top left. *Dendrobium* Hawaiian Gem, p. 230

Top right. *Dendrobium* Muang Thai, p. 230

Bottom. *Dendrobium nobile* hybrid Fortune 'Love', p. 230

Opposite left. *Epidendrum atroniceum*, p. 232

Opposite right. *Epidendrum cinnabarinum*, p. 232

Odontocidium Mackenzie Mountains, p. 241

Odontioda Grouse Mountain, p. 241

Lady Slipper *(Paphiopedilum* Niobe*)*, p. 242

Lady Slipper *(Paphiopedilum* Psyche*)*, p. 242

Phalaenopsis Baguio, p. 243

Renanthopsis Shalimar, p. 244

Opposite. *Phalaenopsis* Marion
Fowler 'Talisman Cove', p. 243

Oncidium Sum Lai Woh, p. 241

Mokara Madame Panni, p. 224

7. EXOTICS: COMPLEX, UNUSUAL SHAPES AND COLORS

Bird of paradise *(Strelitzia)*
Bromeliad (flower stalks, foliage vases of genera such as *Aechmea, Ananas, Guzmania, Neoregelia, Tillandsia, Vriesea)*
Gingers (including *Alpinia, Costus, Hedychium, Tapeinochilos, Zingiber)*
Heliconia
Kangaroo paw *(Anigozanthus)*
Lotus, including seed pod *(Nelumbo)*
Passion Flower *(Passiflora)*
Pineapple lily *(Eucomis)*
Protea (including related *Banksia, Dryandra, Grevillea, Leucodendron, Leucospermum)*
Telopea

Right. *Telopea speciossissima*, p. 247

Opposite.
Top left. Mini Pineapple *(Ananas comosus variegatus)*, p. 222
Top right. Ornamental banana *(Musa ornata)* 'Banana Royale', p. 240
Bottom. Bromeliad *(Aechmea fasciata)*, pp. 162-164

Right. Kangaroo paw
(Anigozanthus hybrid), p. 223

Opposite.
Clockwise, from top left:
Butterfly Ginger *(Hedychium
flavum)*, p. 235;
Red Ginger *(Alpinia purpurata)*,
p. 221;
Beehive Shampoo ginger
(Zingiber spectabile), p. 249;
French Kiss ginger *(Costus
spicatus)*, p. 228;
Red Ginger *(Alpinia purpurata)*,
p. 221.

Page 152.
Bird of Paradise *(Strelitzia
reginae)*, p. 247

Page 153.
Top row, left to right: *Heliconia
magnifica; Heliconia lingulata
'Southern Cross'; Heliconia
rostrata.*
Bottom row, left to right:
Heliconia champneiana 'Mayan
Gold'; *Heliconia orthotricha* 'Edge
of Night'; *Heliconia* 'Golden
Torch'.
See p. 236

Top left. *Calathea platystachys*, p. 225
Top right. Pineapple lily *(Eucomis comosa)*, p. 233
Bottom. Passion flower *(Passiflora 'Incense')*, p. 243

Opposite.
Lotus *(Nelumbo nucifera)*, p. 240

Top left: *Leucodendron* 'Lenox', p. 238
Bottom left: King Protea *(Protea cynaroides)*, p. 244

Opposite. Top row, left to right: *Protea nerifolia* with pods of *Eucalyptus teragona*, p. 244; *Leucodendron discolor* male below, female above, p. 238; *Leucospermum reflexum*, p. 238. Bottom row, left to right: *Dryandra formosa*, p. 231; *Banksia coccinea*, p. 225; *Leucospermum tottum* 'Pink Star', p. 238.

Right.
Phalaenopsis Zuma Happiness flutters above a base of caladium leaves and vertical accents of broom. Inside the bamboo vase a recycled olive jar filled with water keeps this 30-inch-high arrangement fresh.

Opposite.
Tropical foliage grown in Hawaii is a suitable background for many brightly colored flowers. The foliage shown here includes yellow striped pandanus, flat green Ti *(Cordyline)*, bold whale-back *(Curculigo)*, arching *Chrysalidocarpus* palm, and upright tropical *Lycopodium*.

5.
DECORATIVE FOLIAGE:
Favorite Types of Leaves

Few flower arrangements are complete with flowers alone. In this chapter, you will be introduced to some of the more interesting and adaptable of foliage plants, so that you can learn to enhance the beauty of floral arrangements with greenery.

Traditions and Experiments

Foliage is the natural background for flowers. A plant's normal leaves are always appropriate with its flowers, although creating contrast with botanically different foliage is a popular artistic option. A classic example of this arrangement is using the traditional ferny foliage of *Asparagus setaceus* as a background for roses. Fronds of leatherleaf fern (*Rumohra*) are popular behind carnations as a contrast to shape and color.

Some foliage is so dramatic that it can stand alone as an arrangement. Examples include many of the variegated types of *Pandanus*, *Dracaena*, and gingers. Brightly colored leaves of the croton (*Codiaeum*) and Ti leaf (*Cordyline terminalis*) can hold their own with bold tropical colors of anthuriums, heliconias, and flowering gingers.

Traditionally, florists selected particular types of foliage because they lasted well, were easily grown, and provided suitable backgrounds to popular flowers. In recent years we have a much broader range of foliage

159

At a San Francisco wholesale florist various foliage is offered: ferns, asparagus plumes, bear grass, lemon leaf, and huckleberry.

available, because of rapid air transport from tropical regions where much of the more colorful material is grown. Experiment with any foliage that catches your interest. Although you may not often see coleus or dieffenbachia leaves in common arrangements, such colorful foliage lasts well when cut and works nicely in some designs.

A general artistic rule is to choose foliage that helps your flowers look best. This approach explains why most designers choose shades of green leaves rather than multicolored foliage as a backing in designs.

Look to your houseplants for interesting foliage. Create miniature arrangements with a sprig of foliage and a purchased flower or two. A few stems of bargain-priced, short-stem roses, for example, look delightful with bold leaves from scented geraniums or in a modern design with upright tufted fronds from a foxtail fern (*Asparagus densiflorus* 'Meyers').

160

Grasses

You can incorporate an airy feeling into your designs by using grass foliage and seed heads. The tall, upright types such as zebra grass (*Miscanthus sinensis* 'Zebrinus') provide useful height, texture, and sometimes color interest. Variegations occur as speckles and stripes; some grasses are even red or yellow. Innovative florists will offer unusual grasses along with more traditional foliage choices. You can find wild grasses free for the picking along roadsides or in vacant lots almost anywhere. For a ready supply of stems from late spring into fall I like to grow a few grasses in the garden.

Preserving Foliage

Grasses and most other leaves can be kept flexible when dried if you preserve them with a solution of glycerine. Mix 1 part of glycerine with 2 parts of very hot water. Stir or shake until the water and glycerine are blended. Cut off ½ to 1 inch of stem before placing the stems in a vase of the solution. To avoid having the water foul, I add a floral preservative.

Let the stems absorb the glycerine solution for several weeks, until you feel the leaves becoming slightly slippery from the absorbed solution. Once the leaves have absorbed this solution they can be dried yet will

Popular houseplants may be used as foliage in fresh flower designs. This selection includes (top, left to right) *Aglaonema, Chamaedora* palm, *Caladium* 'Candidum', *Dieffenbachia,* and (bottom, left to right) *Araucaria* pine, *Syngonium,* and English ivy (*Hedera helix* cultivar).

161

remain flexible. This is the basic procedure used to preserve eucalyptus leaves, often with a dye added to tint the foliage.

Proteas and banksias also dry nicely with this absorption technique. To keep some color in the flower bracts of proteas, mix water-soluble food color or florists' flower dye into the water-glycerine solution.

Tropical Foliage Care

Leaves from tropical plants last best if kept at temperatures above 50° F. A few, such as caladium and alocasia, should be kept at an even warmer 60° to 65° F to avoid discoloration from the cold. Leaves with a heavy shiny substance, such as philodendron, monstera, croton, and bird of paradise, can be shined with a light coating of mineral oil. The oil also helps to slow water loss through leaf pores.

Thin tropical leaves often last longer if given a soak in warm floral preservative before being used in an arrangement. For example, you can harvest mature caladium leaves from a well-watered plant, then submerge the entire leaf and stem under warm water for a few hours. The same treatment is useful for alocasia leaves. Avoid soaking leaves that have a powdery silver (glaucous) coating. Water and oil may damage glaucous leaves such as those of dusty miller, or some succulents, such as *Kalanchoe fedtschenkoi*.

Bromeliads

Relatives of pineapples, bromeliads are tropicals often grown in pots as plants. They are seldom sold as florist foliage or cut flowers, yet they are useful for both. The exception, a true pineapple, the miniature variegated *Ananas* sold as a decorative accent, has tennis-ball-sized fruit tufted with spiny leaves in white, green, and pink stripes.

Bromeliads are most often available as houseplants, and are useful for their foliage as well as their flower stalks. These genera include *Aechmea, Guzmania, Neoregelia, Tillandsia,* and *Vriesea,* and all need several years to reach flowering size. After only one blooming, the rosette sprouts a

Above.
An easily assembled table decoration features gloxinia flowers with three hybrid caladium leaves in a clear vase.

Opposite.
Aechmea fasciata (top)
Neoregelia carolinae 'Tricolor' (bottom)

few offsets before dying. Another 1 to 3 years passes before these small plants will bloom. Showy species are 1 to 2 feet tall and 1 to 2 feet wide. Because of their size and slow growth, bromeliads are not usually grown for use as cut flowers or foliage.

Even so, bromeliads are suitable subjects for designs as cut flowers or as stiff leaves or whole rosettes placed as foliage accents. Since many genera are epiphytic plants, adapted to living on tree branches with the roots holding onto bark and the inner rosette of leaves filled with water, these types may function as living vases for cut flowers. Bromeliads most often seen at florists and garden centers as growing plants are:

AECHMEA

The silver vase plant, *A. fasciata* is a 12 to 24-inch-tall species with small blue flowers peaking out of bright pink bracts. A cut inflorescence usually lasts at least 10 days in water. *A. fulgens discolor albomarginata* has 10 to 12-inch wine-green leaves with white stripes. The small flowers turn into red and blue berries.

GUZMANIA

Most have glossy green or bronze leaves and red to orange bracts held above the foliage.

NEOREGELIA

Grown for variegated or red-blushed rosettes, the ½-inch blue or white flowers appear just above the water inside each rosette. A favorite cultivar is *N. carolinae* 'Tricolor' which has creamy, striped leaves that blush a deep red when the plant is ready to bloom.

TILLANDSIA

This genus consists of many species varying from Spanish moss (*T. usneoides*) useful for soft, hanging, silvery foliage, to showy flowered species with yellow to red bracts on 1 to 3-foot spikes. *T. ionantha* grows as a 1 to 3-inch ball of silvery leaves which blush red. This tiny species is often sold growing on sticks or tree fern, and, as such, makes an interesting addition to tropical designs.

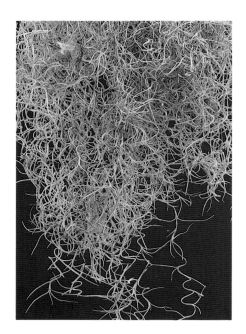

Spanish moss (*Tillandsia usneoides*)

VRIESEA

Called flaming sword, this genus has 1 to 2-foot-tall spikes of orange to red bracts from which appear small yellow flowers. Striped or blotched foliage on popular *V. hieroglyphica* and *V. splendens* dramatizes arrangements. Cut flower spikes last well fresh or as dried accents.

Winter Holiday Greens

Trimmings from the traditional Christmas tree make good background greens for fresh holiday flowers. I avoid hemlock for indoor use since it drops needles in a few days under normal home conditions. The best choices are fir, spruce, pine, and yew. The flat fronds of arborvitae (*Thuja*) and plume false-cypress (*Chamaecyparis* cultivars) are also charmingly different, long-lasting choices.

Other cold-hardy winter holiday choices include ivy (*Hedera*), holly (*Ilex* cultivars), *Pieris*, and mountain laurel (*Kalmia*). I find these greens last longest when given a coating of antitranspirant spray after being soaked in a warm floral preservative solution. Evergreen leaves sprayed with a coating such as Wilt-Pruf have a fresh, glossy, wet look. The coating slows water loss through leaf pores so the greens last longer. To help your greens stay fresh follow these steps:

1. Cut stems at an angle.
2. Plunge stems to a depth of 6 to 10 inches under lukewarm water containing a flower preservative.
3. Keep the stems soaking for 24 to 48 hours in a room at 40° to 50° F, away from sun and dry, hot air.
4. Spray all surfaces with an antitranspirant solution.
5. Use a floral preservative in the water for your arrangement.
6. Place the arrangement in the coolest possible location. If you are giving a party, consider keeping the arrangement in a cool, shady place until it is time to decorate. Flowers and greens do best under cool, humid conditions.

Selecting Fresh Foliage

At the florist look for well-colored, rather tough foliage. Leaves that are thin and tender will not last long in arrangements. Some foliage is sold attached to part of a root; asparagus, for example, may be pulled out rather than just cut. Foliage with an attached stem such as *Monstera*, philodendron, rhizomatous begonias, and Ti *(Cordyline)* stem tips may actually root in your arrangement water.

Such vigor leads to a very long-lasting foliage display, which perhaps will serve as background for several rounds of cut flowers. I used a tall *Sansevieria* leaf in an arrangement in July. By early fall it had rooted, and by January it was sprouting new shoots from within the kenzan dish.

In the following pages I list 41 of the most popular and useful foliage plants, most of which you will find at well-stocked florists' shops. Although we have not illustrated all the other types of foliage available, I encourage you to explore this exciting field by trying such leaves as begonia, papyrus *(Cyperus)*, *Dracaena*, many genera of ferns (use fully mature fronds), evergreen *(Euonymus)*, holly *(Ilex)* with or without berries , *Leucothoe*, *Osmanthus*, ripe fronds from any unusual palms, *Polyscias*, and trailing pothos *(Scindapsus)*. For inspiration visit your local florist to check over a live assortment of foliage. Even more exciting is an early-morning trip to a major wholesale florist, where a variety of beautiful leaves is usually on display.

Some wholesale dealers will be happy to have you as a customer if you are willing to buy bunches of 10 to 25 stems, which is how the leaves come packed from growers. Otherwise just look, learn, and then ask your local retail florist to order the leaves you like best.

A bromeliad, *Vriesea carinata* X *V. fenestralis* hybrid, has yellow flowers sprouting from colorful bracts.

165

Aglaonema commutatum

Alocasia Sedenii

Common Names

Many florists and customers prefer to use popular or common names for plants rather than the more precise scientific names of genus, species, and cultivar or hybrid designation. To help you find what you want I have listed many common and popular names. If your florist gives you a blank look when you ask for *Asparagus asparagoides*, just request smilax.

AGLAONEMA

commutatum cultivars
Common name: Chinese evergreen
Colors: green mottled with silver or creamy yellow
Aglaonemas are 1- to 2-foot-tall tropical plants often grown indoors for their silver-marked leaves and clusters of yellow to red fruit. Stems show dormant root stubs that quickly grow into active roots if a cut stem is put in water. Various cultivars offered as houseplants differ according to the extent and pattern of silver leaf color. Many plants in tropical Asian habitats grow in deep, moist shade. In cultivation aglaonemas survive low light without problems. Use rooted stems of Chinese evergreens as long-lasting backgrounds for cut flowers. Add ¼ teaspoon water-soluble fertilizer per gallon of water for a solution to keep aglaonema stems healthy for months.

ALOCASIA

cuprea, macrorrhiza, odora, watsoniana; hybrids
Common names: Elephant's ear, ape leaf, or taro (*A. macrorrhiza*)
Colors: green, variegated white
Alocasias are tropical aroids, very similar to species of *Colocasia*, which are also called elephant's ear and taro. Alocasias include some metallic-leaved ornamentals such as *A. cuprea* and the striped hybrid 'Amazonica', both bold accents in any arrangement.

AMPELOPSIS

brevipedunculata; cultivar 'Elegans'
Common name: Ampelopsis
Colors: green, variegated white
This relative of the grape is useful outdoors as a vine to cover walls or the bare ground. My favorite is the 'Elegans' cultivar, which has lots of white in the leaves, pink stems, and light blue berries in the fall. Stem lengths of ampelopsis vine are nice for a trailing line. Leaves will last 5 to 7 days in water; the berries will last longer.

Ampelopsis brevipedunculata

Araucaria heterophylla

ARAUCARIA

araucana, heterophylla (A. excelsa)
Common names: Monkey-puzzle *(A. araucana),* Norfolk Island pine
Color: green
The Norfolk Island pine is best known as an evergreen houseplant. Outdoors in mild or tropical climates these trees mature at 200 feet. Florists may offer densely needled flat branches of *A. heterophylla* or, less commonly, the spiny blue-green branches of *A. araucana* (use gloves!). I like *A. heterophylla* as a potted plant indoors; *A. araucana* is less graceful but makes dramatic shadows when lit from the side or below; it offers ample space between rough branches for fresh flowers to show if used in arrangements.

Artemisia 'Powis Castle'

ARTEMISIA

absinthium, ludoviciana, schmidtiana; cultivars
Common names: Wormwood, dusty miller
Colors: green, silver
The felted silver-gray leaves of popular cultivars look nice with flowers of any color. One of my favorite wormwoods is the cold-hardy cultivar *A.* 'Powis Castle', whose cut stems last at least a week in arrangements.

ASPARAGUS

cultivars of *asparagoides, densiflorus,* and *setaceus*
Common names: Smilax, foxtail fern, emerald fern, ming fern, plumosa fern, sprengeri fern
Color: green
Vining smilax is *A. asparagoides.* Ming is a branched, tufted type of *densiflorus myriocladus;* the fluffy asparagus fern plumosa is a form of *A. setaceus. A. densiflorus* 'Meyers' has a fluffy "foxtail" look, sometimes with orange berries. *A. densiflorus sprengeri* has needlelike leaves and tiny thorns. *A. asparagoides,* which florists call smilax, comes in two types, cultivated—often trained by twining stems together—and wild collected stems. The cultivated type is far easier to use in arrangements. A bunch of cultivated smilax may be 3 to 4-feet long. I like to cut it in half for smaller arrangements. If you cut the long stems, keep track of which end is the lower part so that you will place the proper end in the water.

AUCUBA

japonica cultivars
Common name: Japanese laurel
Colors: green, variegated yellow
Aucuba foliage resembles that of a croton plant but with less of a color range. Most popular are the cultivars with lance-shaped, spotted yellow leaves, as seen in 'Crotonifolia' and 'Variegata' (sometimes called gold dust plant). Aucuba is a useful houseplant, and I have had aucuba leaves last more than 8 weeks in an arrangement.

BUXUS

microphylla japonica and *microphylla koreana* cultivars; *sempervirens*
Common names: Korean boxwood, Japanese boxwood, English Boxwood; Oregonia (variegated)
Colors: green, variegated yellow, variegated white
The English box (*B. sempervirens*) comes in plain green and variegated types; the Oregonia of the florists' trade is variegated. Buxus has woody stems and small, deep green leaves. *B. sempervirens* has a strong woody scent. Some Korean and Japanese box cultivars are cold-hardy to -10° F. New hybrids combine *B. koreana* and *B. sempervirens.* A reasonable substitute for boxwood in arrangements is the boxwood holly, *Ilex crenata.*

CALADIUM

bicolor hybrids
Common names: Angel wings, elephant's ear, caladium
Colors: multicolored
Popular caladiums have multicolored leaves, some matte, others very thin and parchmentlike. A few types such as 'Candidum' and 'Aron' are green and white, so they combine with flowers of any color. The pink and red caladiums look nice with bold orchids. Soak the leaves in water a few hours before arranging.

CAREX

morrowii 'Variegata'
Common name: Japanese sedge grass
Color: variegated white
This evergreen, perennial, cold-hardy sedge from Japan grows a neat 10 to 12-inch mound of arching, grassy leaves, in green striped with white and often with a yellow tinge. I find that cut leaves last at least a month. The arching, tapered leaves add an airy feeling to arrangements. If you grow Japanese sedge grass, harvest by pulling leaves from the center of a clump.

CHAMAEDORA

elegans, Neanthe bella, oblongata
Common names: Bella palm, commodore fern, Xate
Color: green
The flat fronds of *Chamaedora* are easy to ship and popular in designs; cut exports of Xate from Guatemala earn the Central American country over $2 million per year. This compact palm is a favorite houseplant and as such a good source of occasional fronds for your arrangements.

Far left.
Asparagus setaceus

Left.
Aucuba japonica

Far left.
Variegated Boxwood
(*Buxus sempervirens*
'Albo-marginata')

Left.
Caladium 'Red Flash'

Far left.
Carex morrowii 'Variegata'

Left.
Chamaedora elegans

CHLOROPHYTUM

comosum cultivars
Common name: Spider plant
Colors: green, and green with stripes of white or pale yellow
Chlorophytums are popular as adaptable indoor plants often grown in hanging pots to show off the trailing runners dotted with rosettes of plantlets. This strawberry-like habit of producing runners bearing plantlets makes chlorophytums useful as a source of foliage for flower designs. Plantlets soon develop roots even while still attached to the runners of their mother plant. Twist off a few plantlets to float in a low centerpiece design or around the base of candlesticks. The plantlets will grow well for months in water, forming a graceful background for cut flowers. In the summer, dot bright red or orange nasturtiums or small marigold flowers between rosettes of spider plants in low dishes, perfect decorations on a patio table.

CODIAEUM

variegatum pictum; many cultivars
Common name: Croton
Colors: multicolored
Crotons are popular outdoor shrubs in tropical regions and as indoor plants for bright humid locations. Leaf shapes and colors range from the thin, narrow, gold-marked *Punctatum aureum* to old oak-leaf hybrids with multicolored foliage in red, yellow, and pink. Crotons are useful as whole stems or single leaves.

COLEUS

blumei and *pumilus* hybrids
Common name: Flame nettle
Colors: multicolored
This familiar houseplant comes in a wide range of color combinations from green and white through orange to deep red. Leaf size and stem length vary; the largest are

Spider plant (*Chlorophytum comosum*)   Croton (*Codiaeum*) hybrid   *Coleus* hybrid

les of the Valley and foliage (*Convallaria majalis*)　　Ti hybrid 'Compacta Royale' (*Cordyline terminalis*)　　Whale-back leaves (*Curculigo*)

6-inch leaves on 36-inch stems. Pick short stem sections from a growing tip. The stem will often root even as the leaves contribute to your arrangement.

CONVALLARIA
majalis and cultivars
Common name: Lily of the valley
Colors: green, variegated yellow
I like the stiff upright leaves of lily of the valley as background foliage, especially the yellow-striped cultivar 'Aureo-variegata'. In the fall, blueberry-sized red-orange fruit forms on 4 to 6-inch stems; the berries are also useful in arrangements.

CORDYLINE
terminalis; many cultivars
Common name: Ti leaf
Colors: green, multicolored, variegated yellow, variegated white

Tropical Ti plants grow as small shrubs, often with a single, stiff, central stem. The foliage varies from curly to broad, flat, and lance-shaped, and leaves range in size from a few inches to 2 feet. Some cultivars are at their best when grown where nights are cool—usually on mountain slopes in the tropics. Growers offer whole tips of stems and single leaves. Flexible Ti leaves are favorites with designers who enjoy braiding and layering leaves.

CURCULIGO
capitulata
Common name: Whale-back palm
Color: green
This broad, 3 to 4-foot leaf looks very much like a palm, but *Curculigo* is in a different family. I prefer to use whale-back leaves to create a cavelike shelter for flowers, or as a dramatic vertical accent behind equally bold tropicals such as heliconias or gingers.

171

Sago (*Cycas revoluta*) Shield fern (*Dryopteris erythrosora*) Pothos (*Epipremnum aureum*)

CYCAS
revoluta
Common name: Sago palm
Color: green
Sago palms are slow-growing, long-lived conifer relatives with palmlike leaves sprouting from a central crown. I like glossy fresh fronds of the Sago with bold, bright flowers. Sago leaves can be gently twisted into circles, then tied with wire. Once dry they will stay in the circular format and leaves turn a soft beige or yellow. Leaves of the Florida Coontie (*Zamia floridana*), which are similar but shorter, are also used in the florist trade.

DRYOPTERIS
erythrosora
Common names: Baker fern, Japanese shield fern
Color: green
Dryopteris produces flat fronds useful for arrangements.

More graceful than common leatherleaf fern (*Rumohra [Arachnoides] adiantiformis*), *Dryopteris erythrosora* is also cold hardy: My plants survive winters with temperatures of -5° F and the fronds still look appealing even after months of snow, wind, and ice. New growth is a colorful bronze-red. Pick mature fronds for best vase life.

EPIPREMNUM
aureum (Scindapsus aureus)
Common name: Pothos
Colors: green, variegated yellow, variegated white
Like the *Monstera* vine, pothos has smaller juvenile leaves but in maturity develops larger foliage with big holes. Florists may offer either the familiar vine form of juvenile pothos, with 3 to 6-inch leaves, or giant 24 to 30-inch foliage from mature plants. Stems from the popular indoor trailing forms are pretty in designs.

Eucalyptus 'Baby Blue' Galax aphylla Lemon-leaf (*Gaultheria shallon*)

EUCALYPTUS

cinerea, perriniana, pulverulenta, tetragona; others
Common names: Gum tree, mallee, 'Silver Dollar',
'Baby Blue', eucalyptus
Colors: green, silver

Eucalyptus is a large genus of Australian trees best known
in the florist trade as a preserved green or fragrant fresh
foliage. The leaves sold on the market are the round
juvenile foliage, which usually has a silvery white coating.
Some preserved types, such as 'Baby Blue' from the Rod
McLellan Company, have a trademarked name. Florists
may offer whole branches with mature foliage and
seedpods, useful for large arrangements or cut up in several
smaller designs.

GALAX

aphylla (urceolata)
Common name: Galax leaf

Color: green

Shiny round galax leaves come from a low-growing
forest plant sometimes used as a garden ground
cover. In the winter sun, the leaves develop a
pleasing bronze blush. Galax leaves last many days
in water. They are 3 to 4 inches across and so form
an ideal background for small spring bulb flowers
or to edge a shallow dish.

GAULTHERIA

shallon
Common names: Lemon-leaf, salal, papoose
Color: green

Florists offer branches of this 3 to 6-foot-tall shrub for
its glossy, 3 to 6-inch leaves. Californians grow
Gaultheria as a bushy ground cover. Mature branches
may have black berries, a favorite with wild birds. This
plant grows wild from southern Alaska into California.

173

HEDERA

helix cultivars, canariensis, colchica

Common names: Ivy, English ivy *(helix)*, Algerian ivy *(H. canariensis)*, Persian ivy *(H. colchica)*

Colors: green, variegated yellow, variegated white

Trailing cultivars of *H. helix* are the most popular ivy. Curly-leaved and needle-leaved types are nice in small designs, while the larger-leaved forms work well trailing out of containers or creating a waterfall design. Freshly cut ivy may root, thus lasting months. The tropical looking *H. canariensis* and *H. colchica* have 5 to 8-inch leaves.

LYCOPODIUM

complanatum, obscurum, taxifolium

Common names: Tree clubmoss, ground pine, running pine

Color: green

Lycopodium is an evergreen relative of ferns with minute, shiny leaves that resemble pine needles. The stems are used as garlands during the winter holidays. Tall *L. taxifolium* is sold in 18 to 24-inch stems. To get small sections of the types used for garlands, just gently unwind the garland wire, soak the stems, and cut to desired length.

MARANTA

leuconeura and *leuconeura* cultivars

Common name: Prayer plant

Colors: green, multicolored

The prayer plant usually folds its leaves at night, but the foliage is still suitable in arrangements. I find that using a clump of several leaves with part of the trailing rhizome is best. The stem will often root so leaves stay fully fresh for the life of an arrangement. *M. leuconeura* cultivars have leaves marked with red and silver.

MONSTERA

deliciosa

Common name: Swiss-cheese plant

Colors: green, variegated white

Above. From left to right: Variegated myrtus (*Myrtus communis* 'Variegata'), *Monstera deliciosa*, Hala leaf (*Pandanus odoratissimus*), *Pachysandra terminalis*

Opposite. From top to bottom: Variegated ivy (*Hedera helix sagittaefolia* 'Variegata'), Ground pine (*Lycopodium obscurum*), Prayer plant (*Maranta leuconeura* var. *erythroneura*)

Mature leaves of *Monstera* may reach 3 to 4 feet. This tropical aroid grows well as a houseplant or outdoors in the tropics. Wash leaves before using, and gently shine them with mineral oil for an appealing glossy look. The thick stems of the vine are marked by leaf scars, making an interesting addition to some arrangements.

MYRTUS
communis
Common name: Myrtle
Colors: green, variegated white
I grow 'Minima' myrtle as an evergreen pot plant, useful for its glossy leaves and fluffy white double flowers. Florists usually offer branches of larger-growing cultivars. 'Variegata' has white-edged leaves. Myrtle leaves have a pleasant, spicy scent when crushed.

PACHYSANDRA
procumbens, terminalis
Common names: Spurge, Alleghany spurge (*P. procumbens*), Japanese spurge (*P. terminalis*)

Colors: green, variegated white
P. terminalis is a common cold-hardy ground cover with evergreen whorls of thick, 2 to 4-inch leaves. 'Variegata' is a white-bordered kind. Creamy flowers appear on short spikes in the spring; the flowers are not very showy but may be useful in miniature designs. Pachysandra leaves are long lasting in arrangements. Use part of the creeping stem with leaves.

PANDANUS
odoratissimus (tectorius), utilis
Common names: Screw pine, hala, Lauhala (Hawaii)
Colors: green, variegated yellow
The gold-striped *Pandanus* is my favorite foliage plant for arrangement. The sword-shaped leaves, 24 to 36 inches, last many weeks in water and make a dramatic vertical statement. A similar impression on a smaller scale can be made with leaves of the cold-hardy garden plant *Yucca filamentosa* 'Gold Sword'. In the tropics *Pandanus* leaves are used to make baskets and thatch.

175

PHILODENDRON

domesticum, scandens, scandens oxycardium, selloum; many hybrids and cultivars
Common name: Philodendron
Color: green
Some philodendron hybrids have purple or reddish-black leaves. Both large leaves with sturdy stems and trailing vine types are useful in cut-flower arrangements. Mature clumps of *P. selloum* have giant 2 to 3-foot leaves with very distinctly cut margins, more uniform than the cuts in *Monstera deliciosa.*

PHORMIUM

tenax
Common name: New Zealand flax
Colors: green, variegated white, variegated yellow, maroon
The leaves of this flax look somewhat like those of *Pandanus* but are softer. Each leaf can reach 8 feet long, although florists' offerings are usually 3 to 6 feet. Several cultivars are available, offering a choice of maroon, green, red-blushed, and yellow or white variegation.

PITTOSPORUM

tobira
Common names: Australian laurel, mock orange
Colors: green, variegated white
This bushy shrub is popular in mild climates as an evergreen hedge, or indoors as a houseplant. Florists often use the yellow-cream variegated form for designs. Clusters of fragrant, ½-inch, yellow flowers appear in the summer. A useful substitute for variegated *Pittosporum* is a yellow or white cultivar of *Euonymus japonica.*

PODOCARPUS

macrophyllus
Common names: Tropical yew, Buddhist pine
Color: green
This evergreen tree is popular in tropical landscapes and as a bonsai subject. The dark green needles and bushy look of the branches make *Podocarpus* useful in many designs. Cut stems are 18 to 20 inches long; if you grow your own, they can be cut to any length. Even a tuft of foliage with 3 to 4-inch leaves is pretty.

RUMOHRA

adiantiformis
Common name: Leatherleaf fern
Color: green
This is the most popular leatherleaf type, used by florists around the world. Millions of fronds are grown in Central America for export and, when mature, the fronds are tough enough to endure being transported in cool cargo ships to Europe.

New Zealand flax (*Phormium tenax* variegated cv.)

Pittosporum tobira 'Variegata'

Philodendron 'Black Carnival'

Podocarpus macrophylla at Ching Chung Koon temple, Hong Kong

Leatherleaf fern (*Rumohra adiantiformis*)

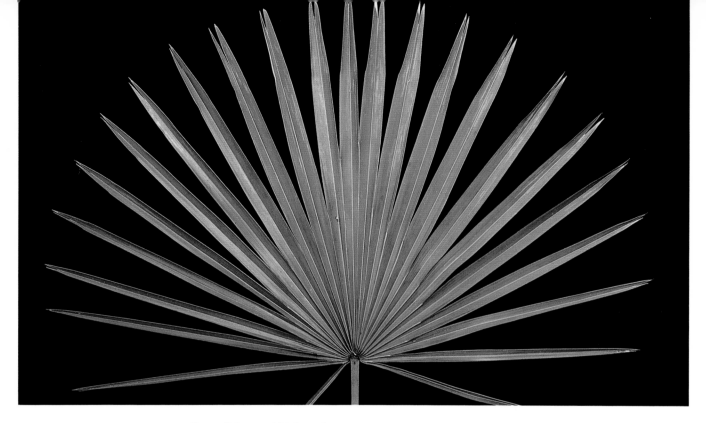

Above. Palmetto (*Sabal minor*)
Bottom left. Dwarf bird's nest (*Sansevieria trifasciata,* 'Hahnii')
Bottom right. *Skimmia japonica* male plant
Pages 180 and 181. *Stromanthe amabilis*
Page 181. Top: Huckleberry (*Vaccinum ovatum*). Bottom: Bear grass
    (*Xerophyllum tenax*)

SABAL

minor, palmetto
Common names: Cabbage palm, palmetto
Color: green
This plant is the most popular fan-shaped palm as a cut green. The smaller-leaved *S. minor*, with 10 to 18-inch leaves, is most often seen, but other species, such as the taller-growing and larger-leaved *S. palmetto*, may sometimes be offered in local markets. Palmettos have fan-shaped leaves 1 to 2 feet across, often with a 12 to 24 inch stem. The clusters of black fruit are also useful in arrangements and may be sold by innovative florists.

SANSEVIERIA

trifasciata; cultivars 'Hahnii', 'Golden Hahnii'
Common names: Snake plant, bird's nest
Colors: green, variegated yellow
This tough succulent, popular as an indoor plant, grows like a weed in outdoor tropical settings so foliage is fairly inexpensive. The dwarf rosette-forming, yellow-variegated 'Golden Hahnii', at 6 to 8 inches, is small enough to be used as a design feature. The tall (6 to 36-inch) forms can look like vertical snakes!

SKIMMIA

japonica
Common name: Skimmia
Color: green
Skimmia japonica is a cold-hardy creeping shrub with male and female plants. Females have hollylike red berries; males have clusters of tiny flowers on short terminal spikes. Both sexes are useful for their evergreen leaves, which are long lasting in arrangements. Stems with leaf clusters may root in arrangements.

STROMANTHE

amabilis
Common name: Stromanthe
Colors: multicolored
This little-known gem is related to the popular houseplants *Calathea* and *Maranta*, and is sometimes sold as *Maranta amabilis*. Stromanthe leaves have interesting purple and silver markings and purple 4 to 8-inch stems. I find that the cut foliage lasts at least 8 days in an arrangement before the leaves begin to curl slightly, revealing purple undersides.

VACCINIUM

ovatum
Common names: Huckleberry, huck, florist green
Color: green
New growth on the huckleberry has a bronze-red blush, while mature leaves are a glossy green on flat twiggy branches. Sometimes you will find small flowers or even fruit, but most branches are sold just for their foliage. Stems are cut 15 to 30 inches long. Wash the foliage before arranging.

XEROPHYLLUM

tenax
Common name: Bear grass
Color: green
The thin, arching leaves of bear grass are useful to add graceful lines to arrangements. I like to tie them in gentle circles or twist the ends around stems or even around a vase. Bear grass lasts 2 to 3 weeks. Florists may sell bunches of short bear grass (to about 30 inches) or the longer kind (up to 50 inches). Longer bundles are best since you can cut the grass to fit your designs. Bear grass is also useful dry; you can preserve it by setting freshly cut stems in a mixture of 1 part glycerine to 2 parts hot water. Stir until glycerine is fully mixed with the hot water. Let the solution cool until it is lukewarm, then put the bear grass in the mixture, stem ends first, to a depth of several inches. As the glycerine is absorbed (after a few weeks) the grass will turn brown. Pour off the solution; the grass will dry but remain flexible.

6.
DESIGNS FOR EVERYDAY PLEASURES AND SPECIAL EVENTS

An awareness of nature is the most important inspiration for successful flower design. Working with fresh flowers and foliage is a relaxing, creative activity, but it may be even more rewarding if one has a knowledge of horticulture. In fact, some of the best commercial designers and successful florists began as students of horticulture.

Basics of Arrangements

Horticulturists appreciate individual flowers for their color, shape, form, and fragrance—all part of natural design. Traditional Western flower arrangements, from lush baroque bouquets to contemporary arrangements combining potted plants with cut flowers, are more complex. Do you prefer an arrangement of three peony flowers (bud, partially open flower, and fully ripe bloom)? Or will you add a background of ferns, blend in contrasting colors with chrysanthemums, and finish off by filling gaps with baby's breath?

Of course, your choice may change to suit the occasion as well as the location of the display. A simple Oriental-style arrangement is exquisite in a plain setting, in front of a beige wall, bamboo screen, plain

Above. With its pot hidden by a natural cork dish, this plant—miniature rose 'Little Liza'—is a delicate, long lasting table decoration.

Opposite. Tree peonies 'Godaishu' (left), 'Higurashi' (center), and 'Ayagoromo' (right) are displayed in a Chinese bowl on top of an antique Chinese picnic hamper. The stems were shortened to 5 inches and placed in a pin holder.

This Victorian-style design features fully developed roses, peonies, alchemilla leaves, and airy grasses held in place by marbles in an antique Venetian vase. In a cool, humid room this arrangement may last four to five days.

mirror, or on an unadorned table. The same arrangement will be visually lost in a complex setting of heavy, carved furniture and multipatterned wallpaper, or in a large room filled with antiques. Japanese styles of flower arranging complement natural shapes and follow the growth patterns, color harmonies, and proportions of nature. It remains for the talented arranger to capture these characteristics in a pleasing design. In the most basic arrangements, only a type of plant material is used, often with a container selected as an important part of the artistic composition.

Whichever style of arrangement you prefer, you will derive maximum pleasure from it when you incorporate appropriate proportions, color harmonies, and balance. But remember to please yourself. All the rules of color harmony, design principles, and artistic compatibility mean nothing if the end result is not pleasing to your eye.

Learn by Observing

Superior flower arrangements and masterpieces of art share attributes, borrowed from nature. Like art academies, flower design schools teach basic principles in great detail. Yet rules in classic Japanese ikebana are so complex that they may spoil the activity as a spontaneous appreciation of nature. So, too, an overemphasis on measurements and color axioms can sour the fun of flower arranging.

I suggest being aware of nature's harmony, without overburdening yourself. Study woodlands and deserts and all the fascinating arrangements in nature. Observations will help you understand harmonious color combinations, pleasing proportion, basic balance, and appropriate blends of form and shape. Fit your arrangement style to the location of your display, the flowers available, and to your own taste.

If you enjoy balance between container and flowers, choose both elements to maintain a relationship of flowers about 150 percent taller (for vertical designs) or longer (for horizontal designs) than the container. If you mix bold flowers with smaller blooms, remember that

Left. This "Famile Rose" flower brick, a museum reproduction of a Chinese container from the Qianlong period (1736-95) is suitable for a horizontal design, as exemplified by this 9-inch arrangement of lacy ivy, miniature rose flowers and -hips, daphne leaves, and 'Fleurette' chrysanthemums. In keeping with the theme, a Chinese rosewood frog and ancient coins were placed nearby.

Below left. Vertical lines of a glossy Bird of Paradise leaf (*Strelitzia*) and a tall calla flower are a striking contrast to richly colored, round clematis, all placed in a low kenzan dish. The 1-inch-tall Burmese sandalwood figure is a balancing note.

Above. *Colchicum* hybrids 'Lilac Wonder' and 'Waterlily' are combined with chrysanthemum 'Donna', which bloom in autumn, in a simple frosted vase to create a relaxed symmetrical design. Adding a touch of color to the base is a string of semiprecious stones.

Creating an asymmetrical arrangement, *Achillea* 'Summer Pastels' hybrids are placed informally in a Thai basket.

the overall arrangement will be more balanced if you keep the larger flowers toward the base of your design.

When deciding on a balance, consider how the composition will fit your display setting. A symmetrical design, with even balance between the vertical and horizontal axes, blends well in formal settings. An asymmetrical design, with uneven balance between horizontal and vertical elements, gives a relaxing feeling.

I prefer asymmetrical balance in most arrangements because my home settings are not formal. A balanced, round, symmetrical arrangement may look lovely as a table decoration yet be ineffective on a summer patio lunch table or casual sideboard.

Center of Attention

Most good arrangements have a center of attention, some portion of maximum beauty or interest. Experienced floral designers strive for a feeling of harmony, balance, scale, and pleasing form. A center of interest

This bold asymmetrical design
features *Hibiscus* 'Lava' and
Caladium 'White Wings'
placed in a small vase behind
the driftwood.

By bending a whale-back leaf (*Curculigo*) in the shape of an arc, the foliage frames a single gladiolus stalk set in foam in a rustic ceramic dish with accents of natural stone. This simple design was inspired by ikebana ideas.

is usually an especially beautiful shape, a color, or a contrast.

When designing an arrangement I place the largest branch or flowers first, creating a structure or foundation. Once the main vertical and horizontal lines are established I may or may not fill in with appropriate material to complete the design. Sometimes I envision an arrangement; at other times, the material at hand inspires improvisation.

Ikebana

The Japanese school of floral design, ikebana, broadly translates as "bring flowers to life." Traditional ikebana designs symbolize heaven above, mankind in the center, and the earth beneath. With most schools of ikebana, seasonal suitability is an important element. Some of my designs draw upon the ikebana traditions yet are free of the historical restraints mentioned in ancient texts.

Some ikebana designs are very sparse and stiff, but they can still provide inspiration for more relaxed designs. Some of the basic ikebana ideas are related to a universal acceptance of balance and harmony.

Most viewers, for example, will enjoy a composition—whether it is a flower arrangement or a photograph—that places the main subject slightly off center; just to the left, right, up, or down, from the actual center of your frame. (This rule is called the "rule of thirds.") In flower arrangements, especially with ikebana, this design principle is often applied. Like so many other rules, however, the rule of thirds is one to break when you have something different to say, or a reason to restate or reinterpret what people expect.

Shifting Impressions

The personality of flowers changes with shifts of light, angle, surroundings, and perspective. As a photographer I know that the quality and direction of light can change a personality. The same is true for arrangements of fresh flowers. Create a bouquet of carnations, view them by a window in direct sun. The impression will be vibrant, shadows

An informal summer
bouquet for a luncheon,
by designer Barry
Ferguson, welcomes
guests on a tree-shaded
patio. The cottage
arrangement includes
zinnias, celosia,
scabiosa, and grasses.

Flower show displays,
such as this lovely
centerpiece of Snowball
Viburnum opulus and roses,
may provide inspiration
for designs.

direct and harsh, the mood fresh with light colors, stirring or passionate with reds. The same flowers seen on a cloudy day foster a pensive mood, and may look romantic, or even sad.

Artificial light also influences the personality of fresh flowers. Some flowers and a few dramatic arrangements may look best with strong, direct lighting; but I prefer soft lighting for most arrangements because it offers open shadows. Having details in the shadows allows us to appreciate each flower, to admire the complex beauty of nature.

In contrast, an arrangement placed in a white room, for example, may have maximum impact with strong lighting that throws dramatic shadows on nearby walls. With strong directional lighting, the shadows join with the flowers to make a final total impression.

Colors influence the impression flowers make on our mood. Yellow captures attention, red invokes passion, pink relaxes, purple looks regal, green and brown provide soft earthy backgrounds to show off brighter colors. In designing your arrangements choose colors to suit your desired mood. You are the director, the creator. If colors please you, use them. If a shape or line appeals to you, it is right for your design.

Floral Design

To start working on your own flower designs, search for ideas in flower shop windows, magazines, at flower shows, and wherever you are likely to find flower arrangements created by experienced designers. Although you may be inspired by someone else's creation, your final arrangement will be an expression of your individual taste and ability. Your choice of colors, flowers, and accessories will ensure that your design is very much your own.

Mechanics

Like students of fine art, who must learn how to mix paints, hold a brush, choose an angle, or create shadings, the flower arranger must master certain mechanics in order to realize an artistic vision. The first of the mechanics is the material—both the plants and the props. Often I

am inspired to create a design by the types of material available. Delicate spring flowers may cause me to search for a small silver or crystal bowl and lace. Huge, brightly colored helicionias call for massive containers, perhaps accompanied by an object from a journey to a tropical country.

The mechanics of basic flower arranging are easy to master. Your artistic vision may require manipulation of materials and supports, but modern floral foams (see chapter 2), container designs, tapes, and pin holders (kenzan) make it simple to keep stems in place. Once mastered, the mechanics will help you achieve artistic success. By learning how to hold a wide range of materials in many types of containers you can realize your artistic floral fantasies.

It is difficult, for example, to get a horizontal line just by placing stems in a vase. If you stuff a container with floral foam, keeping foam ½ to 1 inch higher than the container's edge, you can secure stems at an angle. Use foliage, flowers, or accessories such as driftwood or moss to hide the foam.

Marbles, Pebbles, and Crystals

Holding stems steady in a clear container can be tricky. Fill a tall container about one-third full with something aesthetically pleasing— plain glass marbles blend well in crystal vases, giving some support to stems without distracting the eye from the flowers. Some designers use shallow glass dishes with a pin holder glued inside. Other useful choices are gravel, stones, beads, and shells. If you prefer to use marbles as a design element you might choose those with color.

If you are holding stems in a taller container and do not have enough attractive filling, put a chunk of foam or crumpled chicken wire in the vase center, thus filling much of the space. Now pour the decorative material between the vase and your central mass. This technique helps a limited supply of decorative fillings fill large vases.

After arrangements fade, pour the marbles, pebbles, or stones into a kitchen strainer. Soak them in hot, soapy water, then rinse and dry

Above. A rooted clump of *Acorus gramineus* 'Ogon' provides a long-lasting background for delicate mini-spray roses in a recyclable jar filled with marbles that provide a design element as well as support.

Opposite. Clear marbles are decorative and useful for supporting stems. This arrangement consists of fragrant Lily 'Le Reve' and feverfew (*Chrysanthemum parthenium*). 'Le Reve' is a recent hybrid bred from the Japanese species *L. auratum* and *L. rubellum*.

Soaking sheet moss in warm water makes it flexible enough to wrap around an Oasis mini foam holder. After the plastic holder is hidden, the flower stems may be inserted through the moss into the wet foam, here forming the base for hibiscus.

them. Very large marbles can be put in a wire basket and cleaned in a dishwasher. Inexpensive pebbles or gravel can be recycled on garden paths or as a mulch.

Stability

To keep heavy stems stable, secure a heavy, lead-base pin holder inside the container using putty, waterproof double-sided florist's tape, or silicone caulking. It is important to make a stable base if your arrangement will be moved around. When more bottom weight is needed, you can add pebbles, marbles, or ornamental rocks such as crystal chunks for weight and bracing.

To keep stems from shifting, you can run small strips of clear tape over the top of the container. Keep floral foam from breaking up by wrapping it in ½-inch mesh chicken wire. Tape, wire, foam, and other mechanical supports are easy to hide with foliage, flowers, or sheet moss.

To make a stable base for driftwood, cactus skeleton, or other heavy vertical objects, set the bottom in 4 to 6 inches of plaster of Paris. Hold small sections of wood with screw-in lead weights sold at flower accessory shops or from some mail-order sources listed in the appendices.

Waterproof double-sided tape holds a heavy kenzan pin base (above) inside an antique silver teapot displaying miniature *Cymbidium* Mary Pinchess 'Del Rey' with various foliage— variegated ginger leaves *(Alpinia zerumbet)*, 'Fluffy Ruffles' fern, and *Polyscia guilfoylei* 'Victoriae'.

This Japanese lacquer box serves as an ideal container for a 17-inch-tall design set in a heavy kenzan dish. The arrangement consists of Solomon's Seal and chrysanthemums. Also included here is tea flower (*Camellia sinensis*) placed on a stone found on a beach.

Opposite.
Top. A four-legged Chinese teapot from the Qianlong period (1736-95) makes an interesting container for a flower arrangement. This heavy metal kenzan pin holder fits inside.

Bottom. Even a small piece of Scotch Magic Tape is useful to hold stems in a design; however, waterproof tape is best for use with solutions.

Pin Holders (Kenzan)

Kenzan—a metal-pin flower holder—is a basic tool in Japanese ikebana arrangements; its usefulness is not lost in Western-style arrangements either. Pin holders come in various sizes and shapes; the most adaptable are those with a heavy metal base (often lead) and very sharp, durable brass pins. Pin holders made of plastic shift or topple easily, unless the bases are glued or taped inside a container. Metal kenzan are less likely to shift, but even so, I recommend using double-sided waterproof florist's tape, florist's clay, or tile caulking to hold the base steady in the bottom of a container.

Some containers solve the problem by incorporating metal pins into a waterproof well. The best of these containers are made of solid metal, adding further stability, even for tall stems. My favorites are of plain black (which does not detract from the flowers) and come in several sizes, from plain, round, 2-inch sizes up to a square 9 inches. They are imported from Taiwan by a firm called Two's Company; the basic black color goes with everything, but of course you can customize them by using metal paint.

Tapes

Various kinds of tapes are useful in supporting stems. Green floral tape, or stem wrap, is commonly wound around delicate stems to give added support, sometimes in combination with thin florist's wire. Stem wrap stretches and sticks to itself but is not very strong. I use it to hold and hide wet cotton on corsage stems.

Clear waterproof tape works well for holding stems together in controlled designs; you can also criss-cross it over the top of a container to make an almost invisible grid that will keep stems upright. Double-sided waterproof tape is most useful to secure pin holders in containers or to hold small decorations in place. Before applying waterproof tapes, make sure the surface is dry and free of grease or oil; press the objects together firmly.

Practical tools for flower arrangements include water tubes, clear floral tape, wire in various gauges, and stem wrap. Also handy are sticks to support such stems as this calla and to hold raised water tubes when short-stemmed flowers are placed at the tops of designs.

Common household mending tapes, especially matte-finish Scotch Magic Mending tape, is useful when making grids over container tops, or to hold several stems together above the water. Even inexpensive masking tape makes a useful grid or temporary stem holder. For maximum flexibility and durability under wet conditions, use tape formulated for floral design work. You will find such tape at florists' supply stores and at some sources listed in the appendices.

Wire Mesh

A useful vase filling when you need stem support is wire mesh ("chicken wire") in sizes of ½ to 1 inch. Green, plastic-coated chicken wire, sold for flower arranging, is attractive and less likely to scratch than ordinary wire. You can make a gently crumpled ball of wire, stuffed into your container for support, or place the wire over the top of the container to hold heavy stems in place. Wire mesh also works well when wrapped over bricks of floral foam, to add strength when heavy stems might shift or crack the foam.

Wire Stem Holder and Stems

One metal device for flower design looks like a hybrid between chicken wire and a kenzan. The weighted base, similar to a kenzan base, has bent metal wires; the wide openings of the rounded wire braces are more flexible than the brass kenzan pins. If you use a wire stem holder, secure it to the base of the container to keep heavy or very tall arrangements from wobbling or toppling.

Florists often gain design control by winding thin-gauge green wire around or into short or weak flower stems. You will find handy packs of cut wire in various thicknesses at many shops in botanical gardens, florists' supply stores, and from mail-order sources. Use the thinnest possible wire, choosing the thickness according to each flower stem, to minimize the risk of having the wire detract from the arrangement.

To create an orchid corsage, you should select a mature cattleya.

Top row, left to right: Pull down the sheath to show the first flower that bloomed, then trim the sheath if it is in the way. Using a clean razor or sterile knife to avoid spreading disease between plants, cut the flower off where it meets the inflorescence stem. Place the cut stem in lukewarm water for a few hours before creating the corsage. Here the orchid is in a vase on a tray with supplies needed to create a corsage.

Bottom row, left to right: After several hours wrap a small wad of wet cotton around the cut stem. Cover the cotton with waterproof tape. An alternative to tape is a small piece of self-sticking food wrap or clear plastic. Next, cut a section of flexible aluminum foil to wrap over the tape (commonly used foil colors are gold, green, or blue), then cover the orchid stem with foil.

199

Left. As a final touch, add a long pearl-topped corsage pin so that your orchid can be worn.

Below. Water tubes with rubber caps keep orchid flowers fresh. Small tubes with pins (top left, right, and bottom) are designed so that a cut orchid can be kept in water while being worn as a corsage.

Opposite. A sturdy bamboo stake placed inside a hollow amaryllis (top) will prevent the heavy flower from toppling over in tall arrangements. Trim the stake to the desired height (bottom). Bamboo stakes can be cut an inch or so shorter than the hollow amaryllis stem, then inserted inside to stabilize this heavy flower.

Secure wire to the stem by twisting, then binding with stem wrap tape. You can easily control corsage design with short-stemmed flowers like dendrobium orchids if you push a thin wire up through the flower at the back, bend it over the tip, and pull the wire back down. A bent tip pulled back snugly sticks into the stem, adding stability. With the wire in place, hidden in the bloom, use the lower protruding wire to fashion a false stem. For maximum flower life add a small wad of damp cotton around the stem. Finish the corsage by binding wire, cotton, and stem with green floral tape. Finally, a length of aluminum foil may be wrapped over the tape. Affix a corsage pin so that the corsage may be worn.

Pipe cleaners are also useful to add support to delicate stems. Florists' supply and crafts stores sell dark green pipe cleaners (stem supports) that can be wrapped around stems and almost disappear in an arrangement.

Stakes

Thin wooden stakes are effective when used inside tall, hollow-stemmed flowers, helping to hold them upright in shallow containers. An amaryllis, for example, placed in a shallow container such as a water-well kenzan, might tip unless supported by a thin stake. Cut a thin bamboo stake to fit inside the hollow stem. Be sure the stake is not so tall that it will keep the flower stem from reaching the water. Push the stake into floral foam or into the kenzan pins, and set the hollow arrangement flower on to the stake. Naturally colored tan bamboo stakes or dark green dyed stakes can often be used inconspicuously behind thick stems; several thin stems can be grouped around a stake; use stem wrap to hold them together to surround and hide the stake.

Natural Supports and Perpetual Bases

You can also use the natural structural features of your plant material to serve as supports. The stiff stems of the bird of paradise (*Strelitzia*), for

Amaryllis flowers trimmed from their tall stems are bold accents in some designs, here with Lady of the Night orchids *(Brassavola nodosa),* eucalyptus stems, and the almost-black leaves of a *Begonia boweri* hybrid.

example, are quite sturdy as are a central core of palm fronds, twisted willow stems, contorted hazel branches, or section of heliconia stems.

To create a perpetual base for fresh flowers, use rooted canes of Chinese evergreens *(Aglaonema)*, philodendron, monstera, or similar green-leaved plants that live for years in water. Every few days add some new stems of bright fresh flowers.

The sturdy upright stems of *Aglaonema* give height; arching monstera and philodendron can fill in center areas. Soften container lines and add grace to your design with trailing pothos and *Philodendron scandens*. I find that *Maranta leuconeura erythroneura*, the trailing prayer plant, lives months in water. Its red, silver, and green oval leaves are a pretty color accent. The stems naturally ramble, so they look good trailing over a vase edge. Variegated spider plant *(Chlorophytum)* will also live in water and make trailing stems.

Good long-stemmed choices to add color in your perpetual design are bold gingers, bird of paradise, heliconias, and hybrids of dendrobium and vanda orchids. For some control in placing stems, use clear waterproofing tape in a grid over the container top, intertwine stems, put clear marbles in the vase, or hold stems together with thin florist's wire or green tape.

Your design will change with the season. Around the winter holidays, add cut branches of poinsettia; in springtime, add lilies, glads, and daisies; for fall, choose mums. Remember to pull off from the stems all the leaves that will be under water. Doing this helps keep the water free of rotting vegetation.

To keep your perpetual base plants healthy, add a solution of ¼ teaspoon of water-soluble fertilizer to 1 gallon of fresh water. It is fine to add ¼ teaspoon of fertilizer to each gallon of flower preservative solution as well, thus keeping both the background plants and fresh-cut flowers in top condition.

Specimen Flowers

Full multibloom combinations, traditional arrangements, are only one of

Curly willow branches hold daffodil stems upright while serving as a contrast to the bright yellow flowers placed in a 10-inch-tall nineteenth-century Peking glass vase.

203

A watertight land snail shell from Zululand contains this miniature arrangement of an orchid, a cattleya hybrid (*Slc. Octoberfest*), with Vietnamese anise basil.

many ways to enjoy flowers. As a horticulturist I find single blooms, a flowering branch, or a spike of cymbidiums exceptionally interesting. Learning to enjoy a single flowering stem is easy on your budget.

A single specimen flower in an appropriate container brings pleasure anywhere. Florists often sell flowers by the stem, realizing that contemporary consumers can appreciate individual flowers. Gardeners enjoy cutting prize flowers to admire indoors. Consider creating a special indoor niche—perhaps a shelf with a mirror behind it—as a place devoted to displaying your finest specimen flowers.

You can also experiment by placing a single specimen flower or a spike of orchids in every room. It won't be long before this simple gesture to natural beauty will increase your daily pleasure.

Modest Blooms

A single perfect rose, a voluptuous peony, or a brilliant heliconia is worthy of solo admiration; a modest adornment, however, may complement your overall design. For example a frond or three of fern, *Dicentra* foliage, or a puff of baby's breath *(Gypsophila)* might form the perfect background for a specimen flower.

Choose embellishments to suit your taste. Color combinations, shapely blends, favorite accessories are ideally a personal choice. A modest ornamentation might mean something nonliving. Try draping a necklace or bracelet around a flower stem. Perhaps a favorite piece of driftwood or dry grass plume would complement a proud protea or colorful cattleya orchid.

Thinking Small

Intimate arrangements can be small gems of charming restraint. Some of the Japanese-style flower arrangements feature only a single flowering branch, or branch of foliage balanced by a low mound of chrysanthemums. It is often easier to contemplate the beauty of complex flowers, such as orchids or proteas, by placing only a stem or two in a simple vase. Appreciating flowers is easy when each bloom can be seen.

Keeping arrangements simple has many advantages. Many places around your home will look nicer when graced with a small arrangement of fresh flowers. If you buy your flowers, instead of picking them from a garden, your money will go further when you learn to make each stem do extra decoration duty. Begin by cutting long, multiflowered stems into sections for separate small designs.

A spray of chrysanthemums, for example, can furnish five or six flowers, a frond of asparagus or baby's breath may yield enough sprigs for several arrangements. I find useful material from many houseplants. A stalk or two from an African violet with a frond of fern makes a delightful petite display.

Collect small containers, recycle attractive perfume, medicine, or spice bottles, or build a collection of charming containers for your small designs. Rotate the types of flowers you use and the containers that hold

A simple design idea is to place a single blossom in a small container, such as the ones shown here, which include perfume and wine bottles, recycled jars, and the like. Each little vase takes on a different look depending on the flower it displays.

As an accompaniment for afternoon tea, springtime primroses, a wild dandelion flower, and dicentra leaves are an ideal miniarrangement.

them. Cut floral foam to fit small vases. With water-holding floral foam in place you can position each stem to match your design idea.

Living Centers

Flowering plants are excellent centers for long-lasting floral displays. Using a potted flowering plant is an ideal way to create an enduring decoration for bedrooms, the foyer, bright sun rooms—anywhere, in fact, where a potted plant will survive. For example a potted *Paphiopedilum* orchid, its pot hidden by moss, can be surrounded with cut flowers, each kept fresh with stems in wet floral foam or individual water tubes.

To vary your weekly display surround the potted plant with cutflowers of a complementary color. Chrysanthemums—one of the best cut-flower buys—are available in so many colors that you can change each week's display to suit your mood, a party theme, or decorative motif.

Potted Plants in Arrangements

The poinsettia plants I buy each December provide bright color until at

206

Left. A 4-inch-tall ornate metal stand inspired this miniature design of a sprig of *Ammi majus*, an airy spray of pink *Oncidioda* Robin, *Spathiphyllum* 'Petite', and pink *Hypoestes* leaves. A small clump of *Buddleia crispa* adds fragrance. The flowers stay fresh because they are in a plastic cup with water inside the ministand.

Above. Lily 'Stargazer' shares a platform with long-lasting yellow-spotted *Aucuba japonica* leaves, which have a similar leaf and petal shape. This fragrant Oriental hybrid lily is an international favorite.

least March; occasionally the plants still have their bright bracts when I put them outside in late April. At Halloween and Thanksgiving, it is fun to make an arrangement in a scooped-out pumpkin or ornamental squash. Besides holiday favorites such as poinsettias in the winter, lilies around Easter, and gardenias for Mother's day, I find the following potted plants suitable as focal points for flower arrangements.

African violets (*Saintpaulia* hybrids)
Miniature hybrids are charming when circled with short sprays of baby's breath or cut fronds of fluffy ferns.

Begonias
Old-fashioned wax begonias (*Begonia semperflorens* hybrids) and winter-blooming Reiger hybrids are suitable as flowering plants on their own for long-lasting decoration, or as living centers around which you can create an unusual display of cut flowers. In summertime the spectacular tuberous begonia hybrids provide brilliant flowers in varying forms.

Cyclamen
Newer dwarf hybrids of cyclamen provide at least a month of proud bloom, with silver-mottled leaves under reflexed flowers in white, red, or pink. For an unusual spring arrangement, surround a potted miniature cyclamen with Spanish moss or fern fronds, then add small-flowered daffodils, fragrant hyacinths, or grape-hyacinths (*Muscari*). If you grow houseplants, they will offer a few other flowers to tuck in.

Kalanchoe
This genus of African succulents has been highly bred to produce compact floriferous hybrids now popular during winter months. Red and orange tones are most often seen, but some newer hybrids have yellow, peach, and cream-colored flowers. In a bright cool location, kalanchoes will last at least a month. Let them almost dry at the roots between waterings; the roots rot if kept too wet.

Holiday and Gift Decorations

You can easily customize your holiday decorations by adding unique

Succulent *Kalanchoe fedtschenkoi*, set in a shallow kenzan dish hidden by fragrant pine potpourri, is a sturdy background for brightly colored cosmos. For portability the whole design rests on a straw dish.

To build a festive, long-lasting base for fresh flowers and foliage, a basket (top) decorated with pine cones may be used. Begin by setting an aluminum pan inside the basket, then put a wet section of floral foam (above) in it and place foliage in any desired arrangement. The result is a pleasing design of holiday greens and berries that may be used either with or without flowers. The foliage will last a fairly long time, so different flowers may be used to suit the occasion.

Opposite. While the July 4 holiday inspired this orderly design, other flowers may be substituted for different holidays. Here there are white Moth orchids (*Phalaenopsis*), red and white *Bouvardia*, Columbines (*Aquilegia*), a long-spurred *Angraecum* orchid, and starbursts of *Astrantia major*, all in a handcrafted blue dish.

fresh flowers to purchased products. Around Christmas, for example, most florists, supermarket stalls, and mail-order sources offer very similar evergreen wreaths. One wreath looks pretty much like the next until you add a touch of your own. I like to add fresh flowers to holiday wreaths. Select a flower of your choice. Bright flowers with short stems are most suitable: try adding *Cymbidium* and *Phalaenopsis* orchids, short-stemmed roses (always the least expensive roses), fragrant gardenias, or even small chrysanthemums or miniature carnations. Put each stem into a water-filled, rubber-capped tube, then push the tubes into your wreath wherever you feel a fresh flower would improve the look. Each design can incorporate fresh gardenias, small anthuriums, dendrobium orchids or any other long-lasting fresh flower.

For gift-giving, you can use fresh flowers to add a personal touch to commercially gift-wrapped packages. I like to use cut poinsettias at Christmas. Push the stems into rubber-capped water picks, then use Scotch Magic Tape to fasten the plastic tubes on the wrapped boxes. The tubes can sometimes be

Decorating a special gift package with fresh flowers, in this instance a poinsettia, is easy with the flower stem in a rubber-capped water tube. An orchid or a fragrant carnation corsage may also accompany a gift. As shown here, hide the small water tube under a ribbon, with colored tape, or foil.

held in place by pushing them through a small slit made in wide ribbons, or pushed in among small gifts in baskets.

Combining Flowers with Foliage

As your experience in flower arranging increases, you will develop a sense of how compatible flowers and foliage complement each other. Well-matched partners make a pleasing picture. The artistically appropriate mood is set according to the location and event. What is more, an arrangement for daily home enjoyment needs less care if all living materials have similar lasting qualities.

Designers often create arrangements using flowers that have a similar vase life. Short-lived tulips and anemones, for example, might be combined in a spring arrangement. Majestic designs scheduled for short-term beauty, such as a party or wedding, need not have flowers with a similar life.

If you mix flowers with short, medium, and long vase lives, be prepared to groom your design every day. Pull out any faded flowers and refill containers with floral preservative solution. You may want to rearrange some of the stems to balance the design as short-lived flowers are removed.

Long Lasting Foliage in Arrangements

Sometimes decorative foliage lasts so long that you can use it to complement a succession of flowers. I have had *Aucuba japonica, Galax aphylla, Pandanus,* and *Sansevieria* leaves look perfect for six to eight weeks. Mature lance-leaf *Caladium* hybrid leaves often look nice for a month. Sometimes a *Sansevieria* leaf or *Hedera helix* ivy stem will root, becoming a living plant in your cut flower display.

To help foliage last from design to design, give it an occasional wash. I also trim off ½ to 1 inch from each stem every time the foliage is repositioned in a new design. Of course, you do not need to trim the stems of plants that may form roots, such as ivy, begonias, *Polyscias,*

philodendrons, and *Marantas*. With these easily propagated plants you may have rooted cuttings to pot after bouquet flowers fade.

Natural Displays

The way flowers are displayed influences the effect they have. I like to adjust floral positions to suit nature: If a spray of flowers arches naturally, I prefer to retain the flow in arrangements. The photographs here demonstrate the power of different display styles. Look at the stark,

Above left. Twisted hazel branches, *Caladium* 'Candidum Jr.', and a spider dahlia are held firmly in a metal kenzan dish set on a piece of slate with a sea of dark polished stones.

Above right. *Gerbera* 'Orange Queen' and *Aucuba japonica* form a simple yet pleasing design.

213

upright spray of *Dendrobium* Sonia. The opening bud is intersecting, and the mature flowers make an unusual pattern—yet the natural beauty of the whole inflorescence is lost. However you prefer to arrange flowers, do keep them right side up. Complex flowers such as orchids create a disturbing impression when worn or arranged upside down.

The Color of Light

You can learn to enhance the beauty of your flowers by manipulating the way they are lighted—both by the sun and by artificial means. Although direct sunlight can shorten the vase life of cut flowers, you may feel that the increased beauty is worth the sacrifice. Red flowers, for example, positively glow in red light. You may therefore wish to put your red roses where they will be struck by the light of the early-morning or late-afternoon sun—light that is much more red than the stark sunlight of noon.

You can also change the color of your arrangements by using artificial light. Place a vase of white 'Casa Blanca' lilies or white dendrobiums under a ceiling flood lamp. Keep the lamp far enough away so that the heat won't harm the fresh flowers. The bare bulb will provide sparkling white light. Now put a colored gel between the light and your white flowers; the mood changes. A blue gel creates a mellow, sad mood; pink makes a relaxing glow; and green sets the stage for spooky Halloween pranks.

Another way to change the color of your flowers is with colored lamps. As a photographer I like to use colored gels because they can be changed in a few seconds, but if you want a long-lasting color change just switch the white "normal" bulb with a colored flood lamp. Screw-in lamps come in various colors so you can easily change the mood of the lighting to suit the occasion. Arrangements dominated by white or green flowers are most amenable to artistic changes with colored light. To keep colors natural I use a fluorescent tube that matches noon daylight, such as Naturescent, Vita-Light, or GE Chroma-50. If you want to enrich pink and red tones use a standard Gro-Lux tube.

Mirror Images

Another way to increase your pleasure in flowers is to double it—use mirrors. One living room display in my home uses a long shelf in front of a mirror to reflect each of the flowers on display. An ornamental wooden valance hides a fluorescent lamp below.

Mirrors in bathrooms and in hallways are fine backgrounds for fresh flowers. The mirror adds back light and doubles the number of flowers. Where space permits consider using mirrors under the flowers as well. On a coffee table, for example, or in an entryway, mirrors under the arrangement provide an unexpected perspective, reflecting light into the shadows. Even at your desk, a mirror will provide daily pleasure as it reflects your flower of the day.

You need not spend a great deal of money for mirrors to place by your flowers. Even small mirror sections or the title-type mirrors supplied with double-sided tape are useful as flower multipliers. In addition to increasing the number of flowers on display, the mirrors reflect light to each flower and make small rooms look larger.

Fresh Flowers

Now that you have had an introduction to the art of flower arranging, you are ready to find out for yourself how pleasurable a pastime it can be.

Opposite.
Dendrobium Sonia, an orchid commonly found in florists and markets, is lovely alone or used in combination with other flowers. When its stem is pushed deep into a narrow vase, this orchid (top) looks awkward because flowers are forced into an unnaturally upright presentation. In contrast, the photo below shows the flower in its natural position with its spray arching gracefully from a vase and its flowers facing forward as in nature.

The beauty of roses or other flowers may be enhanced if placed in front of a mirror.

215

A bold *Sabal* palm leaf dramatizes the colorful beauty of hybrid Germini miniature gerberas placed in a Chinese basket.

Browse through the flower portraits—or, better yet, browse at a florist's shop or wholesaler.

Notice the work of the master designers at formal occasions if you need inspiration. Feel free to borrow hints from nature, too. But above all, be ready to please yourself with the serene beauty of fresh flowers and foliage.

APPENDICES

Fresh Flowers Facts Chart

In this chapter you will find facts about the fresh flower types pictured in the preceding chapters and commonly available in the international cut-flower market. The facts listed for each flower type provide general information regarding correct names, colors, seasonal availability, relative costs, vase life, fragrance characteristics, best picking stage, and a general comment including useful details regarding specialized care.

Local florists and regional botanical gardens are a good source of supplemental seasonal facts. Professional florists may also consult their wholesale suppliers for details regarding any of the products offered. Specific hybrids within a genus may vary from market to market, but the care information and other facts remain similar.

Accounts

The chart provides a basic description of each type of flower and a page reference to one or more photos illustrating the type.

Names

Plants are listed under their genus name, a Latinized word; following the genus name are names of popular and readily available species or, in some cases, hybrids or cultivars. To help you become familiar with the group, the family name in English is also given. Most plants have one or more common (English) names as well; the most frequently encountered common names are also provided. In the descriptive paragraph that follows, either kind of name may be used; some generic names, such as *Dendrobium*, are regularly used in place of the "common" name. They are used so often, in fact, that the italics (which signal the use of the scientific name) are frequently forgone. The Latin names may seem difficult at first, but try to learn them anyway, because then you will be speaking the language of the horticultural professionals—and chances are you will gain more respect and find better buys on the market.

Florists typically deal with orchids under broad generic headings, regardless of the complex hybrid background of many cut-flower types. In contrast to most other flower families, orchids are frequently hybridized between different genera, as for example, the common corsage orchid, *Brassolaeliocattleya*. This man-made genus (Blc.) contains species of *Brassavola*, *Cattleya*, and *Laelia*. Generally in the fresh flower markets all hybrids involving the genus *Cattleya* are called "Cattleya hybrids."

Similarly the genus *Vanda* is frequently bred

with related genera to create a range of multi-generic hybrids such as *Aranda, Ascocenda,* and *Mokara.* I have grouped the orchids illustrated here in a similar fashion.

Color

I have listed colors naturally available under each flower type. Florists and suppliers may dye flowers, either by absorption dyes in water, dip dyeing, or sprays. The absorption dyes, when used with restraint, can create unusual colors that look natural, such as deep yellow tuberoses.

You will not find naturally vibrant green carnations nor blue phalaenopsis but florists may use dye to get such colors. My preference is for natural colors, yet I have seen some very pleasing examples of pastel tinting. For instance, a pink tinting to spring broom *(Cytisus)*, normally white and yellow, resembles a cherry blossom in a miniature garden design.

Season

The season given for each flower reflects availability in markets, not just the usual blooming period for each species or cultivar. Popular crops are raised in both the northern and southern hemispheres, but at different times of year. All other factors being equal (market supply, quality, variety, and the like) flowers, like fresh foods, are least expensive in their natural season. Thanks to jet airplanes, Australians can enjoy the fall flowers of the northern hemisphere in the Australian winter. North Americans, in a pleasant exchange, can buy Australian or New Zealand spring flowers when fall frosts slow gardens in the north. When you purchase fresh flowers, it is not always easy to determine their origin except by applying seasonal logic.

Cost

The relative cost lists popular flowers as inexpensive ($), moderately costly ($$), and expensive ($$$). Miniature carnations, at around $4.00 retail per bunch of 25 stems, are inexpensive; a spider chrysanthemum at $1.00 per stem is classed as moderately costly; and a single heliconia or protea at $15.00 is considered expensive. As a general rule fresh flowers and foliage are less costly in their usual season and in local markets. For people in the northern hemisphere, daffodils are inexpensive in March but costly in August.

An excess of product on the market tends to lower prices as dealers push to sell their perishable goods. When fresh flowers are scarce, or demand exceeds supply, the prices rise.

When prices are too high or selections are scarce, remember that less is often more. In the hands of a resourceful artist, a few carefully selected, well-placed stems can make an impression to rival a vase stuffed full of blossoms.

Life

A flower's vase life varies according to many factors (see chapter 2 for complete information about maximizing vase life). In the chart, a flower's vase life is given as short, medium, or long; the rating assumes careful handling from grower to consumer.

Fragrance

Within a genus, the strength and character of the fragrance varies from species to species or cultivar to cultivar. Paperwhite narcissus have a strong perfume, for example, but some other narcissus are only lightly scented. Some cymbidium orchids have a distinctive lemony perfume yet others have no scent. If a specific fragrance is important to you, be sure to mention it when ordering flowers from florists. When you shop in person, just use your sense of smell. In the chart, the fragrances are classified as none, slight, or pronounced.

Picking Stage

The best time to harvest cut flowers is variable. Some flowers do best if harvested when still in the bud stage, others when slightly open, and still others when fully ripe. The chart provides the optimum picking stage (bud, open, or ripe) for each genus.

ACACIA: *baileyana, dealbata, longifolia, retinoides*, p. 120   Pea Family

Feathery-leaved *A. dealbata* is the most popular mimosa. *A. retinoides*, usually sold as 'Floribunda', has thin, leathery leaves and balls of yellow, fragrant flowers. Buy all types with flowers showing color. Mimosa is sold as 15-24-inch flowering branches. Dries easily.

COMMON NAMES	COLOR	SEASONS	COST	LIFE	FRAGRANCE	PICKING STAGE
Mimosa, wattle	yellow	winter, fall	$$	short to medium	slight to pronounced	open

ACHILLEA: *filipendulina, millefolium, ptarmica*; also hybrids and cultivars, p. 127   Daisy Family

Achillea is best known for flat-topped, golden-yellow *A. filipendulina* cultivars, which also make excellent dry flowers. Newer hybrids bring a range of pastel colors to the Achillea palette. These include seed-grown 'Summer Pastels' and the Galaxy hybrids from Germany.

COMMON NAME	COLORS	SEASONS	COST	LIFE	FRAGRANCE	PICKING STAGE
Yarrow	lavender, red, pink, white, yellow	all	$-$$	medium to long	none	ripe

AGAPANTHUS: *africanus (umbellatus), orientalis*; hybrids, p. 91   Lily Family

Agapanthus have 24-36-inch stiff stems with round clusters of light to dark blue flowers. Some whites are also available. Dwarf hybrids such as 'Peter Pan' (blue) and 'Rancho White', which grow 12-20 inches tall, are nice in containers on a sunny terrace.

COMMON NAME	COLORS	SEASONS	COST	LIFE	FRAGRANCE	PICKING STAGE
Lily of the Nile	blue, white	winter, summer	$$	medium to long	none	open

ALLIUM: *aflatunense, giganteum, neapolitanum, sphaerocephalon*, p. 113   Onion Family

The most popular allium is *A. giganteum*, with round, purple flowerheads on 3-4-foot stems. *A. aflatunense* is slightly smaller; *A. neapolitanum* has white flowers on 8-12-inch stems. Any of the alliums are useful in arrangements, even the white to pink flowers of various garlics and onions.

COMMON NAMES	COLORS	SEASONS	COST	LIFE	FRAGRANCE	PICKING STAGE
Garlic, flowering onion	lavender, pink, white	spring, summer, fall	$-$$	medium to long	none to slight	open

ALPINIA: *purpurata, zerumbet*, p. 150   Ginger Family

Alpinia leaves are often used as foliage in tropical designs. Flowering stems at florists are 3-6 feet high, cut from stalks that grow 10-15 feet. *A. purpurata* is purple-red or pink, depending on the cultivar. *A. zerumbet* has hanging clusters of white flowers marked with pink.

COMMON NAMES	COLORS	SEASONS	COST	LIFE	FRAGRANCE	PICKING STAGE
Red or pink ginger (*A. purpurata*), shell ginger (*A. zerumbet*)	pink, red	all	$$	medium to long	none	open

ALSTROEMERIA: hybrids, p. 91   Alstroemeria Family

Modern alstroemeria hybrids are bred for multiple flowering stems, bold colors, and good vase life. The leaves turn yellow easily, so remove as many as possible for each design.

COMMON NAME	COLORS	SEASONS	COST	LIFE	FRAGRANCE	PICKING STAGE
Peruvian lily	blue, pink, lavender, orange, white, yellow	all	$$	medium to long	none	open

AMARANTHUS: *caudatus (hypochondriacus), tricolor*, p. 94   Amaranthus Family

Amaranthus caudatus cultivars have drooping or upright clusters of red or green tightly clustered flowers that look good fresh or dried. Amaranthuses are sold as 1-3-foot stems. Tiny black seeds will fall from the mature *A. caudatus*. *A. tricolor* has red and yellow leaves.

COMMON NAMES	COLORS	SEASONS	COST	LIFE	FRAGRANCE	PICKING STAGE
Love-lies-bleeding (*A. caudatus*), Joseph's coat (*A. tricolor*)	pink, red	summer, fall	$-$$	medium to long	none	open to ripe

AMARYLLIS: (Syn. *Hippeastrum*) hybrids, pp. 74, 94   Amaryllis Family

Amaryllis is the accepted name for these popular bulbs, although some taxonomists feel that *Hippeastrum* is the correct genus name. Up to 4 round, outward-facing flowers appear on 12-24-inch hollow stems. Amaryllises are cut in bud, but only those showing bright color should be purchased.

COMMON NAME	COLORS	SEASONS	COST	LIFE	FRAGRANCE	PICKING STAGE
Amaryllis	orange, red, lavender, pink, white	winter, spring, fall	$$	short to medium	none	bud or open

AMMI: *majus*, p. 121   Carrot Family

Ammi is an annual with slightly larger, more open flower clusters than the wild Queens Anne's lace (*Daucus carota*). Both make excellent cut flowers. The open, airy look and white flowers blend well in mixed arrangements.

COMMON NAME	COLOR	SEASONS	COST	LIFE	FRAGRANCE	PICKING STAGE
Queen Anne's lace	white	all	$-$$	medium to long	none	open

ANANAS: *bracteatus striatus, comosus, nanus*, p. 149   Pineapple Family

The best *Ananas* for indoor decoration are the fruits of *A. bracteatus striatus*, available on 8-10-inch stems. Fruits of the common pineapple are also useful in arrangements for a bold shape. Spiny, stiff, pink-and-white varie-gated *A. comosus*, which are 12-30 inches long, are nice, long-lasting accents.

COMMON NAMES	COLORS	SEASONS	COST	LIFE	FRAGRANCE	PICKING STAGE
Red pineapple, dwarf pineapple	pink, white	all	$$	medium to long	none	ripe

ANEMONE: *coronaria*; hybrids, p. 77 Ranunculus Family

The 'Mona Lisa' strain of 4-5-inch flowers on 15-24-inch stems comes in bright colors with darker centers. Poppy anemone stems curve toward light, the way tulips do. Some double flowers are available. Anemones close at night; they last longest if kept cool with stems in preservative solution.

COMMON NAME	COLORS	SEASONS	COST	LIFE	FRAGRANCE	PICKING STAGE
Poppy anemone	blue, pink, lavender, red white	all	$$	short to medium	none	open

ANETHUM: *graveolens*, p. 120 Carrot Family

Common dill has clusters of tiny yellow flowers, resembling a loose Queen Anne's lace. Florists offer 15-36-inch stems. Fennel (*Foeniculum vulgare*) is similar but with longer lasting, ferny foliage. Dill leaves are popular in cooking and in pickles.

COMMON NAME	COLOR	SEASONS	COST	LIFE	FRAGRANCE	PICKING STAGE
Dill	yellow	all	$	medium to long	none	open

ANIGOZANTHOS: *flavidus, manglesii, pulcherrimus, rufus*; hybrids, p. 151 Kangaroo Paw Family

Kangaroo paws come on 12-36-inch stems with clusters of fuzzy 1-3-inch flowers opening at the tip into a starry shape. The actual flowers do not last long, but the whole fuzzy bud endures many days. New hybrids offer color combinations in red, yellow, and peach tones. A relative, *macropidia*, is called black kangaroo paw.

COMMON NAME	COLORS	SEASONS	COST	LIFE	FRAGRANCE	PICKING STAGE
Kangaroo paw	red, yellow, peach	all	$$	medium to long	none	open

ANTHEMIS: *tinctoria*, p. 77 Daisy Family

Anthemises have 2-inch, bright yellow, daisy-type flowers on 12-24-inch stems. Some hybrids have white flowers with yellow centers. Mix the yellow types with purple cosmos for a charming summer bouquet.

COMMON NAMES	COLORS	SEASONS	COST	LIFE	FRAGRANCE	PICKING STAGE
Yellow daisy, golden Marguerite	white, yellow	summer, fall	$	medium	none	open

ANTHURIUM: *andraeanum, scherzerianum*, p. 95 Arum Family

The anthurium's showy part is a waxy spathe with a stiff, central spadix. Cultivars of *A. andraeanum* are the most popular. Obake types are partially green; tulip types are smaller with partially closed spathes. The twisted spadix of *A. scherzerianum* resembles a pig's tail.

COMMON NAME	COLORS	SEASONS	COST	LIFE	FRAGRANCE	PICKING STAGE
Flamingo flower	pink, red, white	all	$$	long	none	ripe

ANTIRRHINUM: *majus; many hybrid strains, p. 126*   Snapdragon Family

Because snapdragons are raised around the world in gardens and greenhouses, they can be found in the market all year. Stems vary from 10 to 36 inches; florists generally prefer the longer types, but some of the dwarf garden strains are just as nice in small arrangements.

COMMON NAME	COLORS	SEASONS	COST	LIFE	FRAGRANCE	PICKING STAGE
Snapdragon	orange, pink, lavender, red, white, yellow	all	$$	medium to long	none	open

AQUILEGIA: *caerulea, canadensis, chrysantha, flabellata; hybrids, pp. 130, 131*   Ranunuculus Family

The columbine hybrids with long spurs are the most popular, and blue is the favorite color of florists. Pure yellow Rocky Mountain *A. chrysantha* is a charming, 15-24-inch type. In the summer season multicolored hybrids and an occasional double pink 'Nora Barlow' reach many markets.

COMMON NAME	COLORS	SEASONS	COST	LIFE	FRAGRANCE	PICKING STAGE
Columbine	blue, pink, white	spring, summer, fall	$	short to medium	none	open

ARANTHERA (A cross between the genera *Arachnis* and *Renanthera*.), p. 147   Orchid Family

The hybrid James Storie, developed at Singapore Botanic Gardens in the late 1930s, is still the most popular *Aranthera* in markets. Its flowers are smaller and less colorful than those of *Mokara, Ascocenda*, and various *Vanda*s.

COMMON NAME	COLORS	SEASONS	COST	LIFE	FRAGRANCE	PICKING STAGE
Scorpion orchid hybrids	orange, red	all	$$	medium to long	none	open

ASTER: *cordifolius, ericoides, novae-angliae, novi-belgii; hybrids, p. 82*   Daisy Family

Hybrids based on several species are the most popular as cut flowers. *A frikartii* (*A. amellus* x *A. thomsonii*) is a deep blue flower, 2-2½ inches across. The 'Monte Casino' (*A. ericoides*) hybrids and *A. cordifolius* cultivars are smaller and useful as filler in arrangements.

COMMON NAMES	COLORS	SEASONS	COST	LIFE	FRAGRANCE	PICKING STAGE
New England aster, New York aster, Michaelmas daisies	blue, pink, lavender, white	summer, fall	$	medium	none	open

ASTILBE: *chinensis; many hybrids, p. 117*   Saxifrage Family

Astilbe is a favorite in the perennial garden. Fluffy plumes of tiny flowers appear on stems 12-28 inches high. Hold 1 inch of cut stem tip in boiling water for 30 seconds to improve vase life. The 6-8-inch stems of the dwarf *A. chinensis* are good in miniature designs.

COMMON NAME	COLORS	SEASONS	COST	LIFE	FRAGRANCE	PICKING STAGE
False spiraea	pink, white, lavender, red	all	$$	medium	none	open

ASTRANTIA: *major;* cultivars, p. 81 — Carrot Family

Astrantia has an odor reminiscent of musty cloth with overtones of lemon. The scent is not powerful from a distance so *Astrantia* is a suitable flower for mixed arrangements. Some cultivars are solid pink.

COMMON NAME	COLORS	SEASONS	COST	LIFE	FRAGRANCE	PICKING STAGE
Masterwort	pink-white blend	spring, summer	$$	medium	slight	open

BANKSIA: *baxteri, burdettii, coccinea, collina, ericifolia, occidentalis, speciosa;* others, p. 157 — Protea Family

Banksias are protea relatives from Australia. The upright, brushlike inflorescence has hundreds of tiny flowers inside. The leathery foliage is spiny and dramatic. You can enjoy Banksias fresh for 2 to 3 weeks; they will also dry well in the display vase if you withhold water.

COMMON NAMES	COLORS	SEASONS	COST	LIFE	FRAGRANCE	PICKING STAGE
Bird's nest, giant bottlebrush	orange, pink, white, yellow	all	$$-$$$	medium to long	none	open

BOUVARDIA: *longiflora* hybrids, p. 117 — Madder Family

Hybrids developed and grown in Holland are available in all seasons thanks to the Dutch auctions. Some vendors pack an envelope of bouvardia preservative with the cut blooms. Before arranging, place a plastic bag over the flowers and give them a 12-hour drink of preservative.

COMMON NAME	COLORS	SEASONS	COST	LIFE	FRAGRANCE	PICKING STAGE
Bouvardia	orange, pink, red, white	all	$-$$	medium to long	none	open

CALATHEA: *brenesii, crotolifera, leuconeura, platystachys, warscewiezii* p. 64 — Maranta Family

The tropical calatheas are known as colorful foliage plants. I find 4-8-inch-tall trailing *C. leuconeura* is a long-lasting foliage accent in any design. Taller-growing species furnish 2-4-foot stems with colorful bracts and protruding flowers.

COMMON NAMES	COLORS	SEASONS	COST	LIFE	FRAGRANCE	PICKING STAGE
Fuzzy wuzzy, cigar, peacock leaf	orange, red, white, yellow	all	$$-$$$	medium	none	open to ripe

CALENDULA: *officinalis;* many hybrids, p. 86 — Daisy Family

Modern hybrids of the basic orange calendula offer choices in apricot, creamy yellow, and many double types, some with a contrasting red-brown eye. The showy flowers, 3-4 inches across, are borne on 8-15-inch stems.

COMMON NAME	COLORS	SEASONS	COST	LIFE	FRAGRANCE	PICKING STAGE
Pot marigold	orange, yellow	spring, summer	$-$$	medium	none	open

CALLISTEPHUS: *chinensis* hybrids, p. 82   Daisy Family

China asters come in a variety of shapes. Most look like large chrysanthemums, and some have contrasting yellow or white centers. Most stems have several large flowers at the top and several smaller ones lower down. Asters last at least a week in perfection, often longer.

COMMON NAME	COLORS	SEASONS	COST	LIFE	FRAGRANCE	PICKING STAGE
China asters	blue, pink, lavender, red, white, yellow	summer, fall	$-$$	long	none	open

CAMELLIA: *japonica, reticulata, sasanqua, sinensis (Thea)*; hybrids, p. 81   Tea Family

The most popular camellias are the 2-3-inch flowers of the *C. japonica* hybrids. These are usually double but some are single with yellow stamens in the center. The tea plant *C. sinensis* has single, lightly fragrant white flowers, useful in miniature arrangements. Camellias look best floating in a low dish.

COMMON NAME	COLORS	SEASONS	COST	LIFE	FRAGRANCE	PICKING STAGE
Camellia	lavender, red, pink, white	winter, spring	$$-$$$	medium	none to slight	open

CATTLEYA: *aurantiaca, bicolor, granulosa, intermedia, labiata*; hybrids, pp. 134-137   Orchid Family

Most cattleyas seen in flower markets are complex hybrids bred for full shape, bright colors, and seasonal flowering to meet peak demands. Cattleyas are crossed with related genera to make hybrids such as *Brassolaeliocattleya*, *Laeliocattleya*, and *Potinara*. Top-quality cattleya flowers are picked when ripe, then each stem is placed in an individual water tube. Careful growers ship with protective boxes and waxed paper so that the petals arrive unbroken. Display cut cattleyas with stems in water or water tubes for the longest flower life. The leaves are sold as Orca foliage.

COMMON NAME	COLORS	SEASONS	COST	LIFE	FRAGRANCE	PICKING STAGE
Corsage orchid	orange, pink, lavender, red, white, yellow	all	$$$	medium to long	slight to pronounced	ripe

CELOSIA: *argentea* var. *cristata* hybrids; *plumosa* hybrids, pp. 115, 116, 130   Amaranth Family

Celosia hybrids come in dwarf 10-12-inch plants and tall 15-24-inch types. The *cristata* hybrids have heavy, convoluted combs. The *plumosa* hybrids have graceful, feathery plumes. Both sorts dry well. Pull off most leaves for best vase life.

COMMON NAME	COLORS	SEASONS	COST	LIFE	FRAGRANCE	PICKING STAGE
Cockscomb	orange, pink, red, yellow	summer, fall	$	medium to long	none	open to ripe

CHRYSANTHEMUM: *carinatum, coccineum, frutescens, maximum, morifolium;*   Daisy Family
many hybrids, pp. 74, 77, 82

The best-known "mums" are the *C. morifolium* hybrids, which range from 1-inch pompoms to giant spider mums on 36-inch stems. *C. carinatum* hybrids are multicolored annuals. *C. frutescens* cultivars are marguerites, and *C. maximum* hybrids are shasta daisies. *C. parthenium* is the single or double Feverfew.

COMMON NAMES	COLORS	SEASONS	COST	LIFE	FRAGRANCE	PICKING STAGE
Mums; marguerite (*frutescens*), shasta daisy (*maximum*)	orange, pink, lavender, red, white, yellow	all	$-$$	medium to long	none to slight	open

CLEMATIS: *lanuginosa* hybrids, *macropetala, montana, tangutica,* p. 80   Buttercup Family

Clematis are rare at florists' shops because the delicate, flat flowers are short-lived and do not ship well. Many selections are worth growing if you have a garden. For maximum vase life, dip the cut stems in boiling water to a depth of 1 inch for 30 seconds. The flowers look nice in shallow dishes.

COMMON NAME	COLORS	SEASONS	COST	LIFE	FRAGRANCE	PICKING STAGE
Clematis	blue, lavender, pink, white, yellow	spring, summer	$$	short to medium	none	open

CLERODENDRUM: *thomsoniae,* p. 123   Verbena Family

This is a tropical vine well suited to a sunny, warm window. The white and red flowers appear in clusters, often followed by orange fruit. I like the long-lasting white calyx, which ripens to pink in good light.

COMMON NAME	COLORS	SEASONS	COST	LIFE	FRAGRANCE	PICKING STAGE
Glorybower	pink, red, white	spring, summer, fall	$$	medium	none	open to ripe

CONSOLIDA: *ambigua (Delphinium ajacis, D. consolida* hybrids), p. 118   Ranunculus Family

The ferny-leaved larkspur hybrids are charming in mixed designs. Hybrid strains range from compact 1-2-foot stems to tall 4-5-foot types that look very much like standard delphiniums, but with more delicate foliage. *Consolida* is a useful annual for a sunny garden.

COMMON NAME	COLORS	SEASONS	COST	LIFE	FRAGRANCE	PICKING STAGE
Larkspur	blue, lavender, pink, white	all	$$	medium	none	open

CONVALLARIA: *majalis,* p. 108   Lily Family

This charming, fragrant perennial species bears lovely flowers on single 6-8-inch stems; the blooms can be prettily framed by several of the broad, smooth, pointed leaves. There is a double-flowered form, a pink cultivar, and one with striped leaves. Lily of the valley can easily be forced indoors.

COMMON NAME	COLORS	SEASONS	COST	LIFE	FRAGRANCE	PICKING STAGE
Lily of the valley	pink, white	winter, spring	$$	medium	pronounced	open to ripe

COREOPSIS: *grandiflora, lanceolata, tinctoria, verticillata*; hybrids, p. 86 — Daisy Family

The recently developed double-flowered hybrid 'Early Sunrise' is an excellent cut flower. Hybrids of the annual *C. tinctoria* have 1-2-inch yellow or orange flowers with red-brown centers; they look nice in miniature arrangements.

COMMON NAME	COLORS	SEASONS	COST	LIFE	FRAGRANCE	PICKING STAGE
Tickseed	orange, yellow	summer, fall	$	medium	none	ripe

COSMOS: *bipinnatus, sulphureus*; hybrids, p. 83 — Daisy Family

Tall 15-36-inch *bipinnatus* hybrids have ferny foliage and daisylike flowers, some with contrasting center colors or picotee edging. The smaller yellow to orange *sulphureus* hybrids have 6-8-inch stems, good for low dishes and miniature designs.

COMMON NAME	COLORS	SEASONS	COST	LIFE	FRAGRANCE	PICKING STAGE
Cosmos	lavender, red, orange, pink, white, yellow	summer, fall	$	medium	none	open

COSTUS: *megalobractiatus, pulverulentus, scaber, spicatus*; others, p. 150 — Ginger Family

These gingers vary greatly in the color of waxy bracts and flowers. The fanciful popular names originated with growers. Any of the choices help make an unusual design.

COMMON NAMES	COLORS	SEASONS	COST	LIFE	FRAGRANCE	PICKING STAGE
Spiral ginger, kiss of death	orange, pink, red, white	all	$$-$$$	medium	none	open

CROCOSMIA: *masoniorum*; some hybrids, p. 104 — Iris Family

Crocosmias grow like corms much like their larger relatives, gladiolus. Modern hybrids look like small freesias, with bright red, orange, or yellow flowers on an arching stem 15-26 inches tall. Buds open over a period of 6 to 10 days. Pick off faded lower flowers.

COMMON NAME	COLORS	SEASONS	COST	LIFE	FRAGRANCE	PICKING STAGE
Montbretia	orange, red, yellow	summer, fall	$$	medium	none	open

CROCUS: *biflorus, chrysanthus, corsicus, imperati, vernus,* others and hybrids, p. 106 | Iris Family

Favorite early spring flowers, crocuses may be enjoyed in the garden, and, indoors, as potted bulbs. Garden hybrids with 2-3-inch flowers are most common but the 1-2-inch flowers on pure species are a unique flowering plant. I like to pot bulbs (corms) each fall in a shallow bonsai dish, perhaps with a backing of decorative rocks and a small chunk of driftwood. These cold-hardy bulbs need an October to January rooting period, easy to provide by burying the pot in a box outdoors or keeping it in an unheated garage. By mid-January I bring the pots to a sunny window where the 4-6-inch plants soon offer a 5- to 6-day show. Another option is to buy pots of blooming crocuses from your local florist and then, when the blossoms fade, plant bulbs outside in May so they will provide outdoor flowers the following spring. A few species of crocus such as *C. ochroleucus, speciosus, zonatus,* and the Saffron crocus *(C. sativus)* bloom in the fall.

COMMON NAMES	COLORS	SEASONS	COST	LIFE	FRAGRANCE	PICKING STAGE
Spring crocus, and hybrid clone names	blue, lavender, white, yellow	winter, spring	$	brief	none to slight	bud to open

CYCLAMEN: *persicum;* hybrids, p. 105 | Primrose Family

Potted cyclamens are popular indoor gift plants. The newer miniature hybrids have silver marbled leaves and bear 1-2-inch flowers, even in very small pots. I like to use the miniature plants as a feature in dish-garden designs. Add cut flowers and greens with stems in small hidden vases or water tubes.

COMMON NAME	COLORS	SEASONS	COST	LIFE	FRAGRANCE	PICKING STAGE
Cyclamen	lavender, red, pink, white	winter, spring	$$	medium to long	none	open

CYMBIDIUM: hybrids, pp. 138, 139 | Orchid Family

Standard cymbidium bears 10 to 15 flowers, each 3-4 inches across, on sturdy 15-36-inch stems. Miniature hybrids are more profusely flowering, with up to 25 flowers, each 2 inches across, on 15-24-inch stems. Most hybrids have contrasting darker colors on the lips. Only a few are fragrant. Cymbidium flowers—singly or in pairs or trios—make excellent corsages of 1-3 flowers. Major growers (such as Gallup and Stribling in California) package cymbidium corsages in attractive boxes with see-through tops, ready for florists to sell. Cymbidium flowers in compact arrangements will also be seen in similar packages.

COMMON NAMES	COLORS	SEASONS	COST	LIFE	FRAGRANCE	PICKING STAGE
Standard cymbidium, miniature cymbidium	lavender, red, orange, pink, white, yellow	winter, spring	$$-$$$	medium to long	none to pronounced	ripe

CYTISUS: *canariensis* (flowers), *scoparius* (foliage and flowers), p. 117 | Pea Family

Cytisus is a shrubby plant with small flowers, resembling sweet peas, clustered along wiry greenish branches. The yellow and white flowers are sometimes dyed pink. Cytisus can be grown as a houseplant in a sunny, cool location. It will bloom from late winter into spring.

COMMON NAMES	COLOR	SEASONS	COST	LIFE	FRAGRANCE	PICKING STAGE
Broom, florist's genista, Canary Island broom	yellow	winter, spring	$$-$$$	medium	slight	open to ripe

DAHLIA: hybrids, p. 79   Daisy Family

Florists sell long-lasting cut types, but some popular, low-growing cushion hybrids do not last well when cut. For long vase life dip the cut stem in boiling water to a depth of 1 inch for 30 seconds, then let stems soak in cool flower preservative for 6-12 hours before arranging.

COMMON NAMES	COLORS	SEASONS	COST	LIFE	FRAGRANCE	PICKING STAGE
Decorative dahlia, cactus-spider dahlia, ball dahlia	lavender, red, orange, pink, white, yellow	summer, fall	$-$$	medium	none	open

DAUCUS: *carota*, p. 121   Carrot Family

Wild Queen Anne's lace is a perfect addition to informal summer bouquets. The 2-3-foot-tall flowering stems look especially nice with golden rod and blue asters. This perennial wild *Daucus* is seldom cultivated for cut flowers but the slightly more delicate *Ammi* is common in cut-flower markets. In many areas of the country wild Queen Anne's lace flourishes along roads and in vacant fields. When flower clusters are fully ripe they begin to curl inwards, forming a tennis-ball sized green nest, which is also interesting in arrangements.

COMMON NAME	COLOR	SEASONS	COST	LIFE	FRAGRANCE	PICKING STAGE
Wild Queen Anne's lace	white	summer, fall	$	medium to long	slight	open

DELPHINIUM: *belladonna, cardinale, elatum, grandiflorum, semibarbatum*, pp. 74, 132   Ranunculus Family

The most popular delphinium hybrids are bred from *D. elatum.* They have 15-30-inch stems bearing many flat flowers, each ½-1 inch across. Less majestic (and lower priced) are the larkspurs, sometimes called *D. consolida* or *D. ajacis* hybrids but botanically in the genus *Consolida.*

COMMON NAME	COLORS	SEASONS	COST	LIFE	FRAGRANCE	PICKING STAGE
Delphinium	blue, pink, lavender, red, white, yellow	all	$$	medium to long	none	open

DENDROBIUM: *bigibbum, nobile, phalaenopsis*; many complex hybrids, p. 140   Orchid Family

The *D. phalaenopsis* hybrids, popular as cut flowers, have 1-2-foot stems. The *D. nobile* hybrids may be sold as 1-2-foot pseudobulbs, since the flower stems are short. New complex hybrids have curly petals or stripes. A few approach blue but most are white, pink, deep purple, or yellow. Thousands of dendrobium stems are exported daily from Thailand to major world markets. Singapore and Hawaii are also major growing areas for cut-flower dendrobiums. For maximum life, keep the stems in water or water tubes.

COMMON NAMES	COLORS	SEASONS	COST	LIFE	FRAGRANCE	PICKING STAGE
Singapore orchids, pompadour, dendrobium	orange, pink, lavender, white, yellow	all	$$	medium to long	none to slight	ripe

DIANTHUS: *barbatus, caryophyllus, chinensis;* hybrids, p. 77 — Carnation Family

Carnations are hybrids of *D. caryophyllus.* The mini types have branched tops with several flowers per 12-20-inch stem. Hybrids of *D. chinensis* and *D. barbatus* have sprays of single, long-lasting, 1-2-inch flowers. Florists may dye carnations to get green or blue tones. Cut carnations are graded according to stem length and flower size. The highest quality, called "select," have 28-36-inch stems and flowers up to 3½ inches in diameter. The least costly grades, often used in design work rather than for corsages, may have 12-inch stems with 2-inch flowers.

COMMON NAMES	COLORS	SEASONS	COST	LIFE	FRAGRANCE	PICKING STAGE
Sweet William, carnation, Chinese pink	lavender, red, orange, pink, white, yellow	all	$-$$	medium to long	slight to pronounced	open

DIGITALIS: *ferruginea, grandiflora, lanata, purpurea, thapsi,* and hybrids, p. 118 — Foxglove Family

Foxgloves have fuzzy tightly clustered bell-shaped flowers on 1-3-foot-tall spikes. Smaller secondary flowering shoots often appear alongside the main central stalk. Most cultivars have dark spots inside the flowers, creating pleasing contrasts with the dominant colors. *D. purpurea,* the commonest species, is the parent of many improved forms. *D. thapsi* is smaller, usually a clear pink/lavender.

COMMON NAME	COLORS	SEASONS	COST	LIFE	FRAGRANCE	PICKING STAGE
Foxglove	lavender/ purple, pink, white, yellow	summer, fall	$-$$		none	open

DRYANDRA: *floribunda, formosa, quercifolia,* p. 157 — Protea Family

Dryandras look like powderpuffs but are actually rather prickly to the touch, like their protea and banksia relatives. Dryandras are grown in Australia, California, and Hawaii along with other plants in the family. The flowerheads are 2-3 inches across, borne on 12-15-inch stems. Flowers and leaves dry well.

COMMON NAMES	COLORS	SEASONS	COST	LIFE	FRAGRANCE	PICKING STAGE
Golden dryandra (*D. formosa*), oakleaf dryandra, (*D. quercifolia*)	orange, yellow	winter, spring	$$	medium to long	none	open

ECHINOPS: *exaltatus, (E. ritro, E. humilis),* p. 130 — Daisy Family

The round blue globes appear on 15-30-inch stems. Select cultivars such as 'Taplow Blue' have deep color and they bloom all summer into fall. Fresh *Echinops* has a pleasant honeylike scent but the coarse foliage has prickles. Save flowerheads to use as dry accents.

COMMON NAME	COLOR	SEASONS	COST	LIFE	FRAGRANCE	PICKING STAGE
Globe thistle	blue	summer, fall	$$	medium to long	slight	open to ripe

EPIDENDRUM: *cinnabarinum, radicans* (reed-stem hybrids); others, pp. 134-135, 141   Orchid Family

The reed-stem hybrids have ball-shaped clusters of 1-inch flowers on 24-36-inch wiry stems with waxy leaves. *Encyclia* types, grown from plants with pseudobulbs, are sold as 10-36-inch multiflowered stems; the 1-3-inch flowers resemble small cattleyas. Some are fragrant.

COMMON NAME	COLORS	SEASONS	COST	LIFE	FRAGRANCE	PICKING STAGE
Butterfly orchid	lavender, red, orange, pink, white, yellow	all	$$	medium to long	none to pronounced	ripe

EREMURUS: *robustus, stenophyllus;* hybrids, p. 129   Lily Family

Choose spikes with a third to a half of the flowers open. The stiff, 2-3-foot stalks that florists offer are very dramatic toward the back of mixed arrangements. Combine white and yellow eremurus with purple foxglove for striking vertical accents.

COMMON NAMES	COLORS	SEASONS	COST	LIFE	FRAGRANCE	PICKING STAGE
Desert candle, foxtail lily	orange, white, yellow	spring, summer	$$	medium	none	open

ERICA: *canaliculata, (melanthera), carnea, persoluta*, p. 121   Blueberry Family

Potted erica plants are popular around the winter holidays. I like to use them in a low dish, surrounded with fresh-cut spring bulb flowers. The needlelike leaves of erica drop quickly in a dry environment or if the cut sprays are moved roughly. Cut sprays of cold-hardy *E. carnea* cultivars, sometimes available for winter into spring, are nice in low designs for a dining table.

COMMON NAMES	COLORS	SEASONS	COST	LIFE	FRAGRANCE	PICKING STAGE
Heather, heath	lavender, pink, white	winter, spring	$-$$	medium	none	open

ERYNGIUM: *alpinum, amethystinum, giganteum, planum*, p. 122   Carrot Family

Most cultivars of sea holly have metallic, silver-blue tones and spiny foliage on 15-36-inch stems. After enjoying the flowers fresh for 10 days or longer, let them dry and save them for future arrangements.

COMMON NAME	COLOR	SEASONS	COST	LIFE	FRAGRANCE	PICKING STAGE
Sea holly	blue	summer, fall	$-$$	medium to long	none	open to ripe

EUCHARIS: *amazonica (grandiflora)*, p. 89   Amaryllis Family

Eucharis lilies grow from bulbs. Florists offer 15-20-inch cut stems, each bearing 1-4 flowers. The broad foliage, which looks like *Aspidistra*, will last a week in arrangements, but the leaves are seldom sold with the flowers. You can grow this tropical bulb as a houseplant.

COMMON NAME	COLOR	SEASONS	COST	LIFE	FRAGRANCE	PICKING STAGE
Eucharis lily	white	all	$$	medium	slight	open

EUCOMIS: *bicolor, comosa (punctata), zambesiaca*, p. 154 — Lily Family

Eucomis sprouts from underground bulbs. Florists offer 1-2-foot stems with clusters of ½-inch flowers on the top section, usually tipped with a tuft of small leaves; the whole looks somewhat like a pineapple. The rare *E. zambesiaca* has creamy, almond-scented flowers.

COMMON NAME	COLORS	SEASONS	COST	LIFE	FRAGRANCE	PICKING STAGE
Pineapple lily	white, yellow	spring, summer	$$	medium to long	slight	open

EUPHORBIA: *fulgens, pulcherrima, marginata*, others, pp. 130, 133 — Poinsettia Family

The most famous euphorbia is the poinsettia, now available in red, yellow, white, and pink tones. Arching stems of *E. fulgens* come in similar colors but with small flowers (bracts) all along the graceful stem. A few species are useful as foliage in arrangements. All species of *Euphorbia* bleed a milky sap when cut. Let the sap coagulate in water before arranging, cauterize the stem with a flame, or dip it in wood alcohol. I find cut poinsettias last just as well without any special stem treatment.

COMMON NAMES	COLORS	SEASONS	COST	LIFE	FRAGRANCE	PICKING STAGE
Scarlet plume, spurge, poinsettia (*E. pulcherrima*)	orange, pink, red, white, yellow	winter, spring, fall	$-$$	medium to long	none	open

EUSTOMA: *grandiflorum (Lisanthus russellianthus)*, p. 119 — Gentian Family

Choose stems with several open flowers. Buds that open after cutting have weak color and small flowers. Twisted buds and graceful stems make prairie gentian a favorite cut flower. New hybrids such as 'Blue Lisa' and the Yodel series have long vase life and bright colors. Hybridizer Captain Claude Hope, who developed the dwarf 'Blue Lisa', claims it is a good pot plant.

COMMON NAME	COLORS	SEASONS	COST	LIFE	FRAGRANCE	PICKING STAGE
Prairie gentian	blue, white lavender, pink	all	$$	medium to long	none	open

FOENICULUM: *vulgare*, p. 120 — Carrot Family

Use fennel for filler in mixed bouquets or for the ferny foliage. My favorite type is bronze fennel which has red tinged ferny foliage and flat clusters of tiny yellow flowers 3-5 inches across. Fennel is an herb useful in salads and for the anise-flavored seeds. Stems grow to 5 feet tall but tops 12 to 24 inches look fine in designs.

COMMON NAME	COLOR	SEASONS	COST	LIFE	FRAGRANCE	PICKING STAGE
Fennel	yellow	summer, fall	$-$$	medium to long	none	open

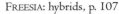

FREESIA: hybrids, p. 107   Iris Family

Modern freesia hybrids are bred for multiple ½- to 1-inch open flowers, large size, and sturdy 1-2-foot stems. Many are fragrant. The best hybrids are multiplied by tissue culture, then plantlets are set in a growing medium to develop the corms that produce the flowers. Most of the cut-flower freesias come from Holland, where they are graded by quality. All of the cut stems are stored in buckets of water in cooled rooms. Growers cut stems that show at least one bud of the cluster in full color, thus being sure that the stem is ripe enough to develop the smaller buds. Freesias are graded by weight. Heavy stems of 22 grams or more are best quality, 16 to 21 grams are most popular in mixed flower arrangements or single color bunches. Smaller stems, as light as 10 grams, are useful in petite designs. Freesia stems are 12 to 24 inches once prepared for the cut-flower market. About 80 percent of all freesias grown in Holland are single types, with white being the most popular color.

COMMON NAME	COLORS	SEASONS	COST	LIFE	FRAGRANCE	PICKING STAGE
Freesia	blue, lavender, orange, pink, white, yellow	all	$$	short to medium	slight to pronounced	open

GARDENIA: *jasminoides* cultivars, p. 78   Madder Family

This shrub, related to the coffee family, produces richly fragrant camellia-like flowers ideal for corsages and striking when floated in a shallow dish. Be sure to handle gardenias gently, because the slightest petal pinch causes a brown bruise. (See chapter 3 for more information about corsage gardenias.)

COMMON NAMES	COLOR	SEASONS	COST	LIFE	FRAGRANCE	PICKING STAGE
Gardenia, Cape jasmine	white	all	$$	medium	pronounced	bud to open

GERBERA: *jamesonii* hybrids, p. 81   Daisy Family

Gerberas last longest when picked after several rows of inner flowers are open but before pollen starts to shed. You can recut the stems to increase vase life. Gerbera stems block easily, so for maximum life cut off at least an inch of stem under warm water every 2 to 3 days. If the flowers have already drooped, cut off 3-4 inches of stem, then hang the flowers on a wire or plastic grid over a container of warm flower preservative, and light from above. After a few hours most gerberas will develop stronger stems. Gerbera stems are sometimes fitted with a plastic cover or twisted wire to keep them straight. New hybrids have stiffer stems. If your gerbera flowers come with protective mesh stockings, gently pull off the stockings so the petals can expand.

COMMON NAME	COLORS	SEASONS	COST	LIFE	FRAGRANCE	PICKING STAGE
Transvaal daisy	lavender, red, orange, pink, white, yellow	all	$$	medium to long	none	open

GLADIOLUS: hybrids, p. 125   Iris Family

Standard gladiolus may be 3 feet tall, while the miniature types, such as *G. colvillei* hybrids, are 1-2 feet. The main seasons are summer and fall. Keep glads upright or the stems will curve. Every day or two, pick off lower faded flowers, then recut the stems to restore balance in your display.

COMMON NAMES	COLORS	SEASONS	COST	LIFE	FRAGRANCE	PICKING STAGE
Gladiolus, glads	lavender, red, orange, pink, white, yellow	all	$$	medium	none	open

GLORIOSA: *rothschildiana, superba,* pp. 90, 93 — Daisy Family

Gloriosa is a vine with flowers on 6-8-inch stems. Florists may offer individual flowers in water tubes or a whole top vine with several clusters of flowers. Choose stems with several fully ripe flowers. Put stems in water tubes to gain height in arrangements.

COMMON NAMES	COLORS	SEASONS	COST	LIFE	FRAGRANCE	PICKING STAGE
Glory lily, gloriosa lily	orange, red, yellow	spring, summer, fall	$$-$$$	medium	none	open

GODETIA: *grandiflora,* hybrids, p. 82 — Evening Primrose Family

Buy or harvest godetias when several flowers are open. Lower buds will open up over a period of days, but blooms close up in the dark. Light and warm water encourage opening. Cut stems under water. Godetias drink a lot of water; be generous, and change the solution of preservative if it gets dirty.

COMMON NAMES	COLORS	SEASONS	COST	LIFE	FRAGRANCE	PICKING STAGE
Clarkia, satin flower	lavender, pink, orange, white	spring, summer	$-$$	medium	none	open

GOMPHRENA: *globosa, haageana* hybrids, p. 128 — Amaranth Family

Gomphrena is best known as a dried everlasting, but the fresh flowers are excellent in arrangements too. New cultivars such as 'Strawberry Fields' (red) and 'Lavender Lady' have bright clear colors on 12-20-inch stems. The lower side flowers may wilt before major top blooms, so cut these smaller stems off and use them in low designs.

COMMON NAME	COLORS	SEASONS	COST	LIFE	FRAGRANCE	PICKING STAGE
Globe amaranth	lavender, red, orange, pink, white, yellow	all	$-$$	medium to long	none	open to ripe

GYPSOPHILA: *elegans, paniculata,* p. 117 — Carnation Family

Baby's breath is popular as an airy filler behind bold flowers and to soften multicolored, mixed bouquets. Pink and white are the natural colors, but florists may dye gypsophila other colors. Buy baby's breath when most of the flowers on the stem are open. Gypsophila dries easily.

COMMON NAMES	COLORS	SEASONS	COST	LIFE	FRAGRANCE	PICKING STAGE
Baby's breath, gyp	pink, white	all	$-$$	short to medium	none	open

HEDYCHIUM: *coronarium, flavum,* p. 150 — Ginger Family

Butterfly gingers are popular in tropical gardens, especially along streams or as clumps in wet places where stems reach 6 feet tall. The 2-3-inch flowers appear in clusters on top of mature stems. Each flower lasts only a day or two but buds continue to open for several days. *Hedychium* stems and foliage are attractive even without flowers and have a fresh ginger scent when crushed. You can grow butterfly ginger as a houseplant, but it will only bloom if given bright sun and warm humid conditions. The stems are sturdy enough to use as design supports for less erect material.

COMMON NAME	COLORS	SEASONS	COST	LIFE	FRAGRANCE	PICKING STAGE
Butterfly ginger	white, yellow	all	$$	short to medium	pronounced	bud to open

HELIANTHUS: *annuus* hybrids, *multiflorus, tuberosus,* p. 87   Daisy Family

Sunflowers are bold, summery flowers. They are usually yellow, but some hybrids have dark centers or white petals. Stems at florists vary from 2-4 feet. The perennial *H. multiflorus* 'Loddon Gold' has long-lasting double flowers. Jerusalem artichoke is the tuberous root of *H. tuberosus,* a species with single yellow flowers.

COMMON NAME	COLORS	SEASONS	COST	LIFE	FRAGRANCE	PICKING STAGE
Sunflower	white, yellow	summer, fall	$$	medium to long	none	open

HELICONIA: *bihai, caribaea, magnifica, psittacorum, rostrata;* others, p. 153   Heliconia Family

Heliconias are tropical relatives of the banana. The bright, waxy bracts hold the actual flowers tucked inside. Stem size varies: *H. psittacorum* cultivars are 1-2 feet tall; *H. magnifica* has pendant flowers on 4-5-foot stems. One or two heliconias can create a dramatic design. Yellow, red, or orange cultivars of *H. psittacorum* are the most often seen because the flowers and 1-2-foot stems are in scale with many designs. Research shows that heliconias with thick stems last longer than those with thinner stems, all other conditions being equal. If you are choosing among any specific type of heliconias and have several stems to choose from, buy the thickest.

COMMON NAMES	COLORS	SEASONS	COST	LIFE	FRAGRANCE	PICKING STAGE
Heliconia, commercial names	lavender, red, orange, pink, yellow	all	$$-$$$	long	none	open to ripe

HELLEBORUS: *lividus (corsicus), niger, orientalis;* some hybrids, p. 85   Ranunculus Family

To retard wilting, dip cut stem end in boiling water for 30 seconds, then soak flowers in lukewarm water for 6-8 hours before arranging. Hellebores last longest in water rather than floral foam. *H. lividus* types have spiny leaves and green to cream flowers in clusters. *H. niger* has white flowers maturing to purple. *H. orientalis* has creamy flowers marked with purple and spotted.

COMMON NAMES	COLORS	SEASONS	COST	LIFE	FRAGRANCE	PICKING STAGE
Christmas rose, Lenten rose, hellebore	green, pink, purple, white	winter, spring	$$	short to medium	none	open to ripe

HEMEROCALLIS: *fulva;* hybrids, p. 93   Lily Family

Each daylily flower lasts only one day but most stems carry five or more buds that open in sequence, one after another. With new flowers opening each day, your arrangement changes, making for an interesting summer display. Daylily stems vary from dwarf forms, at 10 inches, to over 3 feet.

COMMON NAME	COLORS	SEASONS	COST	LIFE	FRAGRANCE	PICKING STAGE
Daylily	lavender, red, orange, pink, white, yellow	summer, fall	$-$$	short	none to slight	open

HIBISCUS: *rosa-sinensis* hybrids, *schizopetalus*, p. 86   Mallow Family

Improved hybrids often last two days, but the normal life-span for flowers is but a day—they open in the morning and close forever at night. I find that branches with buds are worth keeping after the open flowers fade because the buds usually develop to open flowers of somewhat less intense color. The familiar cold-hardy rose of Sharon (*H. syriacus*) is a relative.

COMMON NAMES	COLORS	SEASONS	COST	LIFE	FRAGRANCE	PICKING STAGE
Chinese hibiscus, Japanese lantern (*H. schizopetalus*)	orange, pink, red, white, yellow	all	$$	short	none	bud to open

HYACINTHUS: *orientalis* hybrids, p. 112   Lily Family

Fragrant hyacinths are delightful cut flowers in the cold days of late winter and early spring. The bushy, compact, 8-12-inch stems are made up of many single or double florets. Large bulbs yield heavy full spikes, while flowers from smaller bulbs are less tightly packed and more graceful.

COMMON NAME	COLORS	SEASONS	COST	LIFE	FRAGRANCE	PICKING STAGE
Hyacinth	blue, orange, pink, red, white, yellow	winter, spring	$$	short to medium	pronounced	open

IRIS: *germanica, sibirica, reticulata*; tall Dutch hybrids, p. 109   Iris Family

Summer perennial bearded iris last only a day, but buds open on cut stems for several days. Dutch bulbous iris are the most common all year long at florists' shops. The stems are 16-24 inches. Tiny *I. reticulata* is a fragrant spring bulb flower on 4-8-inch stems; *I. sibirica* hybrids, with 16-30-inch stems, are useful from spring into summer.

COMMON NAMES	COLORS	SEASONS	COST	LIFE	FRAGRANCE	PICKING STAGE
German iris, Siberian iris, Dutch iris	blue, lavender, orange, pink, white, yellow	all	$$	short to medium	none to pronounced	open

IXORA: *coccinea, javanica, macrothyrsa* (syn. *duffii*); hybrids, p. 132   Madder Family

Ixoras are popular as hedge plants in the tropics and as houseplants in colder climates. The clusters of bright flowers resemble geraniums but with many more small blooms. Ixoras look nice in designs of exotics. Try them below towering heliconias or tall dendrobiums.

COMMON NAME	COLORS	SEASONS	COST	LIFE	FRAGRANCE	PICKING STAGE
Flame of the forest	orange, pink, red, white	summer, fall	$$	short to medium	none	open

KNIPHOFIA: *uvaria* hybrids, p. 124   Lily Family

Stems vary from 1-2½ feet, with clusters of flowers at the top. Kniphofias can lend useful height to summer arrangements; cut the sturdy stem short for use in low designs on dining tables.

COMMON NAMES	COLORS	SEASONS	COST	LIFE	FRAGRANCE	PICKING STAGE
Red-hot poker, torch lily, poker plant	orange, red, yellow	summer, fall	$$	medium	none	open

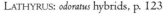

LATHYRUS: *odoratus* hybrids, p. 123   Pea Family

Sold in bunches, sweet peas produce 3 or more flowers on 8-20-inch stems. Old-fashioned types have a pleasant perfume but some modern hybrids are only mildly fragrant.

COMMON NAME	COLORS	SEASONS	COST	LIFE	FRAGRANCE	PICKING STAGE
Sweet pea	lavender, red, orange, pink, white	summer, fall	$$	medium	slight to pronounced	open

LAVANDULA: *angustifolia, dentata, x intermedia, stoechas,* p. 129   Mint Family

The most popular lavenders are *L. angustifolia* selections, but the finely cut leaves of *L. dentata* and large flowers of *L. stoechas* are also useful in summer arrangements. *L. intermedia* is an important source of oil for perfume. Dried lavender holds its color well. I enjoy using lavender to add fragrance to arrangements.

COMMON NAMES	COLORS	SEASONS	COST	LIFE	FRAGRANCE	PICKING STAGE
Lavender, French lavender (*L. dentata*), Spanish lavender (*L. stoechas*)	blue, lavender, pink, white	summer, fall	$$	medium to long	slight to pronounced	open

LAVATERA: *trimestris* hybrids, p. 118   Mallow Family

Lavatera flowers look like miniature hibiscus. The 3-4-inch flowers appear on sturdy 15-20-inch stems. Buy lavatera when several of the flowers are open. The buds will develop and open even after stems are cut. Hybrids 'Mont Blanc' and 'Silver Cup' are easy-to-grow garden annuals.

COMMON NAME	COLORS	SEASONS	COST	LIFE	FRAGRANCE	PICKING STAGE
Mallow	pink, white	summer, fall	$$	medium to long	none	open

LEUCODENDRON: *coniferum, discolor, eucalyptifolium, linifolium, salignum,* p. 156, 157   Protea Family

These shrubs of the protea family provide silvery foliage and colored bracts in yellow, pink, or red. Female branches often have round cones that last for weeks. Some hybrid selections are the red 'Safari Sunset' and 'Silvan Red'. *Leucodendron*s (sometimes spelled *Leucadendran*) are grown in Hawaii, California, and Australia.

COMMON NAMES	COLORS	SEASONS	COST	LIFE	FRAGRANCE	PICKING STAGE
Silver tree, flame tip	pink, red, yellow	all	$$	medium to long	none	open

LEUCOSPERMUM: *catherinae, conocarpodendron, cordifolium, erubescens, reflexum;* cultivars, p. 157   Protea Family

These protea relatives resemble spiny sea urchins; they range from golf-ball size to tennis-ball size. Many cultivars are used in the cut-flower trade, sometimes tinted to deepen the natural yellow to orange tones. Recut stems at a slant and give abundant water, like proteas. *Leucospermum*s may not open well if cut in too tight a condition. Buy flowers that have a bushy, spiny look already, not just a round ball. These flowers may have a slight, pleasant honeylike scent when warmed by the sun.

COMMON NAMES	COLORS	SEASONS	COST	LIFE	FRAGRANCE	PICKING STAGE
Pincushion, sunburst protea, pinwheel (*L. catherinae*)	orange, pink, red, yellow	all	$$	medium to long	none to slight	open to ripe

LIATRIS: *pycnostachya, spicata, (callilepsis)*; hybrids, p. 124   Daisy Family

Liatris flowers appear on stiff, upright stems and look like a purple, pink, or white bottle brush. Flowers open from the top down. Buy spikes with at least 2 inches of flowers open. 'Kobold' is a select dwarf with 15-18-inch stems. Other selections have 24-36-inch spires.

COMMON NAMES	COLORS	SEASONS	COST	LIFE	FRAGRANCE	PICKING STAGE
Gay feather, blazing star,	lavender, pink, white	all	$$	medium to long	none	open

LILIUM: *longiflorum*; hybrids, pp. 88, 92, 93   Lily Family

Fragrant lilies, bred from *L. auratum, L. speciosum,* and *L. rubrum,* are called Oriental lilies; most are white, pink, or white with much red coloring. The Asian hybrids are seldom fragrant; they come in yellow, orange, red, and white. Florists often pull off the stamens so the ripe pollen will not stain flowers or furniture but I think the ripe stamens contribute to the beauty of these flowers. Avoid scattering the pollen on clothing or tablecloths since it will stain.

COMMON NAMES	COLORS	SEASONS	COST	LIFE	FRAGRANCE	PICKING STAGE
Lily, Easter lily (*L. longiflorum* and hybrids); Asian hybrids; Oriental hybrids	lavender, red, orange, pink, white, yellow	all	$$-$$$	medium to long	none to pronounced	open

LIMONIUM: *latifolium, perezii, sinuatum, suworowii, tatarica*; many hybrids, p. 130   Plumbago Family

L. sinuatum is the common statice, with flat clusters of small flowers that look almost the same dried as fresh. *L. latifolium* looks like a cloud of lavender gnats. *L. suworowii* has spires of deep pink flowers on stems that often have interesting twists.

COMMON NAMES	COLORS	SEASONS	COST	LIFE	FRAGRANCE	PICKING STAGE
Statice, sea lavender, German statice (*L. tatarica*)	lavender, red, blue, orange, pink, white, yellow	all	$$	medium to long	none	open

LYSIMACHIA: *clethroides, punctata*, p. 121   Primrose Family

L. clethroides has 3-4-inch spikes of tiny, star-shaped white flowers, each with contrasting pink eye. *L. punctata* has yellow flowers mixed in with small leaves on upright stems 15-24 inches tall.

COMMON NAME	COLORS	SEASONS	COST	LIFE	FRAGRANCE	PICKING STAGE
Loosestrife	white, yellow	summer, fall	$$	medium	none	open

MATTHIOLA: *incana* hybrids, p. 132   Mustard Family

Greenhouse-grown stock is available all year, although the natural season is summer. Pull off all leaves that would be below water in designs. Use flower preservative and add extra bleach if the water becomes odorous. Stocks bear clusters of round, 1-inch flowers on 12-28-inch stems.

COMMON NAME	COLORS	SEASONS	COST	LIFE	FRAGRANCE	PICKING STAGE
Fragrant stock	lavender, red, pink, white	all	$$	medium	pronounced	open

MOLUCCELLA: *laevis*, p. 115 — Mint Family

Bells of Ireland have small white flowers, but the showy part is the papery green cup around each bloom. Spikes somewhat resemble foxgloves. Florists sell 15-30-inch stems. Summer is the natural garden season.

COMMON NAME	COLORS	SEASONS	COST	LIFE	FRAGRANCE	PICKING STAGE
Bells of Ireland	green, white	all	$$	medium to long	none	open

MUSA: *acuminata, coccinea, nana, ornata, sumatrana, velutina*, p. 149 — Banana Family

Banana fruit and foliage from several species may be seen at florists. Most common are the flowering stalks of *M. coccinea* (red) and the pink *M. ornata*. Bananas are heavy and costly to ship, hence these blooms are expensive except in tropical regions.

COMMON NAMES	COLORS	SEASONS	COST	LIFE	FRAGRANCE	PICKING STAGE
Banana, ladyfinger banana	pink, red	all	$$-$$$	medium to long	none	open to ripe

MUSCARI: *armeniacum, botryoides, comosum*, p. 111 — Lily Family

Muscari have clusters of tiny flowers on 4-8-inch stems that grow from underground bulbs. Some cultivars have double flowers. *M. botryoides* comes in blue or pure white. *M. comosum* has a fluffy lavender form called Plumosum. Hold several stems together with a rubber band or thin wire to make the most colorful display in arrangements.

COMMON NAME	COLORS	SEASONS	COST	LIFE	FRAGRANCE	PICKING STAGE
Grape hyacinth	blue, white	winter, spring	$$	short to medium	slight to pronounced	open

NARCISSUS: hybrids, pp. 74, 106, 108 — Amaryllis Family

Although there are many good species of Narcissus that are commonly planted in gardens, most commercially sold kinds are hybrids. After cutting, Narcissus bleed sap that reduces the life of other cut flowers. Therefore you should soak Narcissus stems for 6-12 hours before placing them with other flowers. Narcissus range from about 6 inches to 12 inches or more, and may be single or double. Cut double types after they are fully open.

COMMON NAME	COLORS	SEASONS	COST	LIFE	FRAGRANCE	PICKING STAGE
Daffodil	pink, white, yellow	winter, spring	$	short to medium	none to pronounced	bud to open

NELUMBO: *nucifera*, p. 155 — Waterlily Family

Sacred lotus flowers are a favorite decoration at Buddhist shrines, especially in tropical Asian countries where the plants thrive. Florists in colder areas can import lotus buds from Thailand or Hawaii, mainly as a spring flower, sold wholesale in bunches of 10. The flat leaves, 10-24 inches around, are available more often. Lotus flowers open at night, often to 10 inches across, but generally the flowers are harvested as buds, then formed into rosettes by hand, or just used as graceful buds to decorate shrines. If you see lotus seed pods sold in Asian markets buy one to use as a table decoration, set in clean water with the natural holes holding a few delicate flowers or sprigs of flowering anise basil.

COMMON NAME	COLORS	SEASONS	COST	LIFE	FRAGRANCE	PICKING STAGE
Sacred lotus	light to dark pink, white	mainly spring and summer	$$	short to medium	pronounced	bud

NERINE: *bowdenii, sarniensis*; hybrids, p. 91   Amaryllis Family

Nerine flowers appear in a round cluster atop 10-24-inch stems. Hybrids with bright sparkling colors in pink to deep red are sometimes available as cut flowers, but they are quite expensive.

COMMON NAME	COLORS	SEASONS	COST	LIFE	FRAGRANCE	PICKING STAGE
Guernsey lily	orange, pink, red, white	all	$$-$$$	medium	none	open

NIGELLA: *damascena*, p. 120   Ranunculus Family

Nigella has flat, 1-inch flowers amid very hairy leaves on thin stems. The egg-shaped seed capsules are even more interesting than the flowers. I like to use stems that have already begun to form many seed capsules. Nigella flowers and seed pods work well in dried arrangements, too.

COMMON NAME	COLORS	SEASONS	COST	LIFE	FRAGRANCE	PICKING STAGE
Love-in-a-mist	blue, pink, white	summer, fall	$$	medium	none	open

ODONTOGLOSSUM: *bictoniense, crispum, Odontoglossum* hybrids, multigeneric hybrids   Orchid Family
      (*Odontioda* and *Odontocidium*), p. 142

Odontoglossum orchids bloom on 15-24-inch stems. The popular *O. crispum* hybrids have 2-3-inch round blooms of white, pink, or yellow, often with contrasting brown spots. Complex hybrids with related genera extend colors into oranges and reds and offer new shapes and extended flowering seasons.

COMMON NAME	COLORS	SEASONS	COST	LIFE	FRAGRANCE	PICKING STAGE
Odontoglossum	lavender, red, orange, pink, white, yellow	all	$$-$$$	medium to long	none to slight	ripe

ONCIDIUM: *pulchellum, sphacelatum, splendidum, varicosum*; many hybrids, p. 146   Orchid Family

Most often seen in markets are hybrids such as *O.* Gower Ramsey, *O.* Golden Shower, *O.* Goldiana, which have 1-2-inch yellow flowers on arching 24-36-inch sprays. Miniature hybrids bear tiny flowers, ½-1 inch across on 3-15-inch stems; these come in a wide range of colors. An oncidium on driftwood makes a nice design feature.

COMMON NAME	COLORS	SEASONS	COST	LIFE	FRAGRANCE	PICKING STAGE
Golden shower orchid	lavender, red, orange, pink, white, yellow	all	$$-$$$	medium to long	none to pronounced	ripe

ORIGANUM: *majorana, vulgare*, p. 117   Mint Family

Flowering stems of sweet marjoram and oregano are useful fragrant additions to summer arrangements. The longest-lasting kinds are semiwoody stems of *O. vulgare*, available in shades of white to lavender.

COMMON NAMES	COLORS	SEASONS	COST	LIFE	FRAGRANCE	PICKING STAGE
Sweet marjoram, oregano	lavender, white	summer, fall	$-$$	medium	slight	open

ORNITHOGALUM: *arabicum, thyrsoides*, p. 108   Lily Family

These flowers last longest when kept cool. Buds will open over a period of days. The stems lean toward the light, so turn them daily or pinch out growing tips to keep the stems upright. *O. thyrsoides* has compact 12-20-inch stems; *O. arabicum* has stronger stems, to 36 inches long, and a black-centered bloom. Recent hybrids developed in a breeding program of the U.S.D.A. (Beltsville, Md.) and the University of California at Irvine involve rare species (including *O. dubium* and *O. maculatum*). These new hybrids span a range of warm pastels from cream to orange.

COMMON NAMES	COLOR	SEASONS	COST	LIFE	FRAGRANCE	PICKING STAGE
Chincherinchee, star of Bethlehem	white	all	$$	medium to long	none	open

PAEONIA: *lactiflora, suffruticosa, lutea* hybrids, pp. 79, 80   Peony Family

Most flower-market peonies are herbaceous types, which ship better than the silky-petaled tree peony hybrids. The popular Memorial Day peonies are herbaceous hybrids. Tree peonies are larger and last a few days less. Buy them when they are almost open, with good color showing.

COMMON NAMES	COLORS	SEASON	COST	LIFE	FRAGRANCE	PICKING STAGE
Herbaceous peonies (*lactiflora*), tree peonies (*suffruticosa* and *lutea*)	lavender, red, pink, white	spring	$$	medium	pronounced	open

PAPAVER: *nudicaule, orientale, rhoeas, somniferum*; hybrids, p. 84   Poppy Family

Poppies are delicate as cut flowers but are worth using for their bright colors and charming round shapes. Choose buds just starting to open or recently opened double types. Sear the stem ends over a flame or dip in boiling water for 30 seconds. A few drops of wax in the flower's center will increase life. The dried seed pods of *P. somniferum* are popular for their cupped shape and usefulness in many designs. The poppy seeds used in cooking come from this species; the dried sap from living seed pods is the source of opium.

COMMON NAMES	COLORS	SEASONS	COST	LIFE	FRAGRANCE	PICKING STAGE
Iceland poppy, Oriental poppy, Shirley poppy, opium poppy	lavender, red, orange, pink, white, yellow	summer, fall	$-$$	short to medium	none	bud to open

PAPHIOPEDILUM: *bellatulum, callosum, ciliolare, fairieanum*; hybrids and other species, p. 143   Orchid Family

Paphiopedilum orchids offered at most markets are hybrids bred for round shapes and dramatic colors. Hybrids between two species have more open shapes and look less imposing in arrangements. Orchid specialists may offer straight species and new hybrids with multiflowered stems. Even at the wholesale level, a single paphiopedilum orchid may sell for $8.00 to $10.00, but they are long lasting if fresh. Use these bold orchids as a design feature or accent.

COMMON NAME	COLORS	SEASONS	COST	LIFE	FRAGRANCE	PICKING STAGE
Lady's slipper	pink, red, white, yellow	all	$$-$$$	medium to long	none	ripe

PASSIFLORA: *alata, caerulea, coccinea, vitifolia,* other species, and hybrids such as Alatocaerulea (syn. Pfordtii), and 'Coral Glow', p. 154

Passion Flower Family

For one brief day a passion flower flaunts striking color, intricate structure, and often a seductive perfume. As night approaches the flower slowly folds never to open again. To enjoy passion flowers, grow a vine of *P.* Alatocaerulea, trained on a wire loop, in a sunny window; some florists will supply fresh flowers the morning of a special party. Keep passion flowers open longer with a few drops of wax in the center of each bloom. Place flowers on the lower refrigerator shelf in midafternoon to keep them open until early evening. Some passifloras (such as *P. alata* and *P. edulis*) form edible fruit which yields tropical passion juice. The vigorous hybrid *P.* Alatocaerulea has 4-5-inch blue, pink, and green fragrant flowers; *P. coccinea* and *vitifolia* are red.

COMMON NAME	COLORS	SEASONS	COST	LIFE	FRAGRANCE	PICKING STAGE
Passion flower	blue, pink, lavender, red	summer; all in greenhouse	$$	brief	slight to pronounced	open

PHALAENOPSIS: *amabilis, amboinensis, gigantea, lueddemanniana;* other species and multigeneric hybrids, pp. 134, 135, 144, 145

Orchid Family

The modern hybrids are developed from many different species and genera. *P. violacea* has 1-2-inch fragrant flowers on short stems, characteristics inherited by some of the hybrids on the market. The most popular are pure white, 3-4-inch flowers on arching, 12-36-inch sprays. Pink hybrids are bred from *P. schilleriana. Phalaenopsis* orchids are excellent corsage flowers; florists offer whole sprays with up to 15 flowers or single flowers, usually set in water tubes.

COMMON NAME	COLORS	SEASONS	COST	LIFE	FRAGRANCE	PICKING STAGE
Moth orchid	lavender, red, orange, pink, white, yellow	all	$$-$$$	medium to long	none to pronounced	ripe

PHLOX: *paniculata* hybrids, p. 122

Phlox Family

Phlox are delightful mixed with daylilies in summer bouquets. Try a blend of golden Gloriosa daisies with white and purple phlox. Dip cut stem ends in boiling water for 30 seconds to increase vase life. Pull off most leaves to reduce wilting.

COMMON NAME	COLORS	SEASONS	COST	LIFE	FRAGRANCE	PICKING STAGE
Phlox	lavender, pink, orange, white, yellow	summer, fall	$-$$	short to medium	none to slight	open

PHYSOSTEGIA: *virginiana,* p. 124

Mint Family

The tubular flowers appear tightly along 12-24-inch stems, opening from the bottom up. Even the neatly arranged buds are interesting. Rare variegated clones have pink flowers and stems with white-edged leaves.

COMMON NAMES	COLORS	SEASONS	COST	LIFE	FRAGRANCE	PICKING STAGE
False dragonhead, obedient plant	lavender, pink, white	summer, fall	$-$$	medium	none	open

PLATYCODON: *grandiflorus*, p. 118   Campanula Family

Platycodon is best known for the round, blue flowers that open from balloon-shaped buds. New hybrids have double or single blooms of pink or white, some on short, 10-15-inch stems, others on stems of 12-18 inches. One newly developed kind has buds that never open at all.

COMMON NAME	COLORS	SEASONS	COST	LIFE	FRAGRANCE	PICKING STAGE
Balloon flower	blue, pink, white	summer, fall	$$	medium	none	open

POLIANTHES: *tuberosa*, p. 107   Amaryllis Family

Single and double tuberoses are sold as cut stems of 24-30 inches. Sometimes the white flowers are tinted pink or yellow. Buds have a natural pink exterior tint. Tuberoses, like glads, reach toward the light. Pinch out the top buds if you wish the stems to stay upright.

COMMON NAME	COLOR	SEASONS	COST	LIFE	FRAGRANCE	PICKING STAGE
Tuberose	white	summer, fall	$$	medium to long	pronounced	open

PROTEA: *cynaroides, neriifolia, magnifica, repens;* some hybrids and other species, pp. 156, 157   Protea Family

Proteas are grown in Australia, Hawaii, and California, so there are always a few species available. Make a slanting cut to remove 1 or more inches from the stem. Use a preservative solution and recut stems every few days. Keep flowers dry to avoid rot. Proteas also last well as dried flowers.

COMMON NAMES	COLORS	SEASONS	COST	LIFE	FRAGRANCE	PICKING STAGE
King Protea (*P. cynaroides*), pink mink (*P. neriifolia*)	lavender, red, pink, white, yellow	all	$$$	medium to long	none	open

RANUNCULUS: *asiaticus* hybrids, p. 86   Ranunuculus Family

Modern hybrids have 3-inch, fully double flowers that look like flat carnations or poppies. Spring is the natural season, but growers force crops for the cut-flower market at other times. Ranunculuses will last longest if used as blooming pot plants, but cut stems are also nice in spring arrangements.

COMMON NAME	COLORS	SEASONS	COST	LIFE	FRAGRANCE	PICKING STAGE
Persian ranunculus	lavender, red, orange, pink, white, yellow	all	$$	short to medium	none	bud to open

RENANTHERA: *coccinea, imschootiana, monachica, storiej,* and hybrids, p. 144   Orchid Family

As parents, Renantheras make superior hybrids with such related genera as *Arachnis (Aranthera), Phalaenopsis (Renanthopsis),* and *Vanda (Renantanda).* Renantheras contribute floriferousness and brilliant red to orange colors. When crossed with much larger flowered orchids, such as *Phalaenopsis,* the results are frequently spectacular.

COMMON NAME	COLORS	SEASONS	COST	LIFE	FRAGRANCE	PICKING STAGE
Fire orchid	red, orange	all	$$	medium to long	none	open to ripe

ROSA: hybrids, pp. 76, 96-103   Rose Family

Most of the roses you see at florists are hybrid tea types, bred for perfectly formed, slowly opening buds. Large-flowered roses are graded according to stem length: longer stems bring higher prices, but the 4 or 5 grade levels vary slightly among growers. The usual grades are Fancy, over 26 inches; Extra Long, 22-26 inches; Long, 18-22 inches; Medium, 14-18 inches; Short, 10-14 inches. Less common are miniature roses with 1-2-inch flowers on 10-12-inch stems, usually sold in bunches of 10 stems. Less formal and slightly larger are the Sweetheart or Cluster roses. With access to fresh cut garden roses you can add to this palette various shrub roses, climbing hybrid teas, floribunda and grandifloras, all nice in arrangements but uncommon at cut-flower markets.

COMMON NAME	COLORS	SEASONS	COST	LIFE	FRAGRANCE	PICKING STAGE
Rose	lavender, red, orange, pink, white, yellow	all	$$$	medium	none to pronounced	bud to open

RUDBECKIA: *hirta, fulgida*; hybrids, p. 86   Daisy Family

Gloriosa daisies are cultivated hybrids of the wild black-eyed Susan. Some selections have red-brown centers or prominent green "eyes." Most have 4-5-inch yellow flowers with brown centers on 15-30-inch stems. Gloriosa daisies are easy to grow in a sunny garden.

COMMON NAMES	COLORS	SEASONS	COST	LIFE	FRAGRANCE	PICKING STAGE
Gloriosa daisy, black-eyed Susan, coneflower	orange, yellow	summer, fall	$-$$	medium to long	none	open to ripe

SALVIA: *farinacea, horminum, officinalis, splendens*; hybrids, p. 124   Mint Family

Blue-flowered spires of *S. farinacea* resemble veronica. *S. horminum* 'Claryssa' hybrids have 10-15-inch stems with white, blue, or pink-tinged leaves, a better show than the tiny flowers they hide. *S. splendens* hybrids are loved in summer gardens, and the flowers are also good when cut.

COMMON NAMES	COLORS	SEASONS	COST	LIFE	FRAGRANCE	PICKING STAGE
Sage, Clary sage (*S. horminum* hybrids)	blue, orange, lavender, red, pink, white	summer, fall	$-$$	medium	none to slight	open

SCABIOSA: *atropurpurea, caucasica* hybrids, *stellata*, p. 80   Veronica Family

True blue 'Butterfly Blue' has 2-3-inch flowers on stems 6-8 inches tall, perfect in miniature arrangements. Other cultivars have 15-28-inch stems.

COMMON NAME	COLORS	SEASONS	COST	LIFE	FRAGRANCE	PICKING STAGE
Drumstick (*S. stellata*)	blue, lavender, white	summer, fall	$-$$	medium	none	open

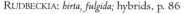

SCILLA: *campanulata, siberica, tubergeniana*, p. 111   Lily Family

The 8-12-inch-tall May flowering *Scilla campanulata* (syn. *Endymion hispanicus, Hyacinthoides hispanicus*) is most often used in spring arrangements. The bell-shaped ½- to ¾-inch flowers are clustered on upright spikes, looking like small, informal hyacinths. Blue, white, and pink cultivars are available, all blending well in spring designs with daffodils or species tulips. The 4-6-inch stems of dark blue *S. siberica* (squill) and light blue *S. tubergeniana* are suitable for mini arrangements. Bunch 6 or 10 stems together when you want a dramatic splash of color.

COMMON NAMES	COLORS	SEASON	COST	LIFE	FRAGRANCE	PICKING STAGE
Blue bells, wood hyacinth	blue, pink, white	spring	$	short to medium	none	open

SEDUM: *spectabile, telephium*, hybrids, p. 130   Crassula Family

Sedums used for cut flowers have 10-18-inch stems with top clusters of starry flowers in pink, white, or bronze-red. The succulent leaves are also attractive, but be sure none rot under water in arrangements. Flower clusters form flat clusters of seed pods if permitted to mature.

COMMON NAME	COLORS	SEASONS	COST	LIFE	FRAGRANCE	PICKING STAGE
Stonecrop	pink, red, white	summer, fall	$$	medium to long	none	open

SOLIDAGO: hybrids, p. 120   Daisy Family

Whether cultivated or wild, goldenrod makes a good cut flower. Its stiff stems, 15-36 inches tall, hold clusters of yellow flowers. The cultivated *Solidago* hybrids, useful airy fillers in arrangements, have slightly larger flowers in a more open arrangement. Solidaster (crosses of *Solidago* with *Aster*) have smaller flowers.

COMMON NAMES	COLOR	SEASONS	COST	LIFE	FRAGRANCE	PICKING STAGE
Goldenrod, Solidaster	yellow	all	$-$$	medium to long	none to slight	open

SPATHIPHYLLUM: *floribundum, wallisii*; hybrids, p. 95   Arum Family

Spathiphyllum is a popular houseplant, appreciated both for its glossy, lance-shaped leaves and snowy white spathes (flowers). The stems may be 10-20 inches long. Compact hybrids with small flowers are good in miniature designs; larger 3-6-inch types are 'Mauna Loa' and 'Lynise'.

COMMON NAME	COLOR	SEASONS	COST	LIFE	FRAGRANCE	PICKING STAGE
Peace lily	white	all	$$	medium to long	none to slight	open to ripe

STEPHANOTIS: *floribunda*, p. 133   Milkweed Family

Fragrant clusters of waxy stephanotises are favorites in bride's bouquets; they also look well floating in a shallow dish. Florists sell individual clusters of 6 to 8 flowers, or sometimes single blooms. Stephanotis is a sturdy vine that can be grown in a warm greenhouse.

COMMON NAMES	COLOR	SEASONS	COST	LIFE	FRAGRANCE	PICKING STAGE
Madagascar jasmine, stephanotis	white	all	$$-$$$	short to medium	pronounced	open

STRELITZIA: *nicolai, reginae*, pp. 75, 152   Bird-of-Paradise Family

The most familiar bird of paradise is *S. reginae*, popular for its dramatic orange petals and deep blue lip atop sturdy 24-36-inch stems. Each flower has several clusters or "birds," but these usually need to be pulled out once the stalk is cut. *S. nicolai* has white flowers.

COMMON NAMES	COLORS	SEASONS	COST	LIFE	FRAGRANCE	PICKING STAGE
Bird of paradise, giant bird of paradise (*S. nicolai*)	blue, orange, white	all	$$-$$$	medium to long	none	open

TAGETES: *erecta, patula*; hybrids, pp. 80, 82   Daisy Family

Dwarf hybrids of *T. patula* are excellent in miniature designs. Larger *T. erecta* hybrids, called American or African marigolds, are bold accents for summer designs. Remove all leaves that might be below water. Large-flowered hybrids have 24-36-inch stems.

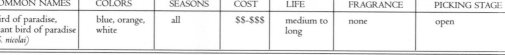

COMMON NAMES	COLORS	SEASONS	COST	LIFE	FRAGRANCE	PICKING STAGE
Marigold, American or African marigold (*T. erecta*), French marigold (*T. patula*)	orange, red, white, yellow	summer, fall	$-$$	medium to long	none	open

TANACETUM: *vulgare*, p. 86   Daisy Family

Tansy has fragrant ferny foliage and ½-inch, ball-shaped flowers in clusters like tiny mums. This flower is suitable for miniature arrangements. Tansy foliage and flower clusters look nice in candlestick holders with blue scabiosa or with pink lilies in a low vase.

COMMON NAME	COLOR	SEASONS	COST	LIFE	FRAGRANCE	PICKING STAGE
Tansy	yellow	summer, fall	$	medium to long	none	open

TAPEINOCHILUS: *ananassae*, p. 64   Ginger Family

Stems of this waxy red Asian ginger are 2-3 feet tall. As with other gingers (*Alpinia, Zingiber*), you can increase vase life by leaving longer stems on cut flowers, because the stems store water. *Tapeinochilus* stems, which have green bands, are useful as decorative accents and supports in arrangements.

COMMON NAMES	COLOR	SEASON	COST	LIFE	FRAGRANCE	PICKING STAGE
Indonesian torch, wax ginger	red	summer	$$	medium to long	none	open

TELOPEA: *speciossima*, p. 148   Protea Family

An Australian shrub, telopea is related to proteas and has an equally dramatic 3-4-inch scarlet flower. This unusual flower is worth ordering for a special dinner party. Set the flower stems in clean water tubes or narrow port glasses buried in an arrangement of exotic fruits, a dramatic way to decorate a dessert buffet.

COMMON NAME	COLOR	SEASONS	COST	LIFE	FRAGRANCE	PICKING STAGE
Warwatah	red	spring, summer, fall	$$	medium	none to slight	open

TRACHELIUM: *caeruleum*, p. 117   Campanula Family

Clusters of tiny flowers appear atop 20-28-inch stems. Blue is the most popular color, but hybridizers have developed new versions in creamy white and pink. Summer is the main season for this species as a cut flower. Try trachelium in tall rustic arrangements with goldenrod and daylilies.

COMMON NAME	COLORS	SEASONS	COST	LIFE	FRAGRANCE	PICKING STAGE
Blue throatwort	blue, pink, white	all	$$	medium to long	none	open

TRITELEIA: *laxa (Brodiaea)*, p. 110   Lily Family

Triteleia flowers appear in clusters and look like a miniature agapanthus. The best-known kind is a cultivar called 'Queen Fabiola'. Since stems are 4-8 inches long, I like triteleias in small to miniature arrangements or mixed in a low vase with yellow flowers.

COMMON NAME	COLOR	SEASONS	COST	LIFE	FRAGRANCE	PICKING STAGE
Triteleia	blue	spring, summer	$$	short to medium	none	open

TULIPA: hybrids, pp. 104, 105   Lily Family

Most tulips offered by florists and garden centers are complex commercial hybrids. Tulip stems continue to grow in water, so the design of an arrangement may change over a period of days. Some markets offer superior large-flowered tulips with extralong stems as "French Tulips." The less costly short-stemmed tulips, 8-12 inches tall, are easier to work with in mixed arrangements.

COMMON NAME	COLORS	SEASONS	COST	LIFE	FRAGRANCE	PICKING STAGE
Tulip	lavender, red, orange, pink, white, yellow	winter, spring, fall	$$-$$$	medium	none	bud to open

VANDA: *coerulea, teres, sanderiana*; many complex hybrids, pp. 134, 135   Orchid Family

Hybrids of the pencil-leaved *Vanda teres* grow like hedges in tropical climates. In Hawaii these bear millions of 1-3-inch flat flowers, which are used in leis. Larger complex hybrids from *V. coerulea, V. sanderiana*, and others offer clusters in various colors on 12-24-inch stems.

COMMON NAME	COLORS	SEASONS	COST	LIFE	FRAGRANCE	PICKING STAGE
Lei orchid	blue, orange, lavender, red, pink, white, yellow	all	$$-$$$	medium to long	none to pronounced	ripe

VERBASCUM: *bombyciferum, chaixii, olympicum, phoeniceum*; hybrids, p. 124   Mullein Family

Mullein plants bear 24-36-inch spikes, often branched, from which the ½-1-inch flowers open. My favorites are the fuzzy, silver-haired types such as *V. olympicum*, whose yellow flowers open over many days. Selections of *V. chaixii* have unbranched spires.

COMMON NAME	COLORS	SEASONS	COST	LIFE	FRAGRANCE	PICKING STAGE
Mullein	pink, white, yellow	summer, fall	$$	medium to long	none	open

VERONICA: *spicata* hybrids, p. 124   Snapdragon Family

Summer is the peak season for veronicas. Cut-flower hybrids have 15-24-inch stems whose wispy spires of tiny flowers give an airy feel in designs. Dip cut stems in boiling water for 20-30 seconds. If the stems wilt, recut them to help the flower take up more water.

COMMON NAME	COLORS	SEASONS	COST	LIFE	FRAGRANCE	PICKING STAGE
Veronica	blue, lavender, pink, white	all	$$	medium	none	open

ZANTEDESCHIA: *aethiopica, albo-maculata, elliottiana, rehmannii;* hybrids, p. 95   Arum Family

We enjoy callas for the lilylike curved spathe; the actual flowers are just tiny spots on a central spadix. *Z. aethiopica* is the largest, often with 36-inch stems. Other species have 15-24-inch stems with 3-4-inch flowers. Use preservative or bleach in the water for arrangements.

COMMON NAME	COLORS	SEASONS	COST	LIFE	FRAGRANCE	PICKING STAGE
Calla lily	lavender, pink, orange, white, yellow	all	$$-$$$	medium to long	none	open to ripe

ZINGIBER: *spectabile*, p. 150   Ginger Family

Like their *Heliconia* and *Alpinia* relatives the shampoo ginger flowers appear inside waxy bracts. These colorful bracts make a dramatic statement in tropical designs. In colder climates you may have to place a special order in advance to purchase *Zingiber* flowers from florists. The 8-12-inch bract cluster looks like an open pine cone on top of a 2-4-foot stem. *Z. officinale* provides the rhizomes so popular in Asian cooking as a flavoring, but the yellow-green flowers are seldom seen. Try sprouting a ginger root that you buy at a market. After 8-10 weeks in moist soil or peat moss the sprouted rhizome stalk should furnish a unique focal point for a miniature design, which would complement a table featuring Asian food.

COMMON NAME	COLORS	SEASON	COST	LIFE	FRAGRANCE	PICKING STAGE
Shampoo ginger	pink to pale red, yellow	summer	$$	medium	none	bud to open

ZINNIA: *elegans* hybrids, p. 80   Daisy Family

Zinnias are favorite summer-garden flowers, now offered in hybrids of every color but blue. Stems range from 6-8 inches on the smaller kinds and up to 36 inches. I like the big, shaggy, cactus types for summer bouquets. Button-type hybrids are nice in miniature bouquets.

COMMON NAME	COLORS	SEASONS	COST	LIFE	FRAGRANCE	PICKING STAGE
Zinnia	lavender, red, orange, pink, white, yellow	summer, fall	$-$$	medium	none	open to ripe

Mail-Order Sources of Flowers and Supplies

The best way to select fresh flowers is to visit your local florist. I like to see, smell, and even gently touch flowers when I'm deciding which to buy. Looking over a display of fresh flowers also gives me ideas about combinations for new arrangements. Visiting a flower shop keeps one in touch with what is in season, how flowers are priced, and what colors look best together.

Sometimes the flowers you want are not available locally. The same may be true of supplies for growing plants and arranging flowers. Ordering supplies and flowers by mail is convenient. To be sure of quality and satisfaction, send your orders to firms that guarantee their products.

Once you start to enrich your life with fresh flowers you will always look for something beautiful. Searching catalogs for flowers and plants is an exciting hobby. If you have a garden, you already know how important mail-order firms are for unusual seeds, plants, and supplies. Even without an outdoor space you can grow flowering and foliage plants in an indoor garden.

Whatever your desire and resources, you will find catalog sources useful supplements to local shopping. The firms I list here are selected to give you a broad choice for supplies and flower types.

American Nurseryman Publishing Co.
111 North Canal St.
Chicago, IL 60606-7276
The firm offers a free catalog of floral books and videos from many publishers.

Anthuriums International Inc.
14 Dunbar Dr.
West Windsor, NJ 08691
Wholesale and retail grower/broker/shipper selling a broad range of tropical flowers. Offerings include orchids, heliconias, anthuriums, and proteas. Flowers grown at numerous farms on different islands of Hawaii and the Caribbean are marketed by this firm, often with direct Federal Express shipping from grower to final customer.

Dorothy Biddle Service
Greeley, PA 18425-9799
This family business was started in 1936 to help flower arrangers obtain the supplies required for complex designs. The firm now sells mainly to wholesalers, but will sell retail if you cannot obtain their products from a local retail shop.

W. Atlee Burpee & Co.
300 Park Ave.
Warminster, PA 18974
Burpee's free catalog of plants and seeds includes some flower-arranging supplies.

Calyx and Corolla
1550 Bryant St., #900
San Francisco, CA 94103
The free catalog offers many fresh-cut flowers, sent via Federal Express. Some arranging supplies are available as well. You can order foliage and wreaths according to the season and for traditional holidays.

Capability's Books
2379 Highway 46
Deer Park, WI 54007
A free catalog includes books about flower arranging, design styles, and many aspects of gardening. Capability's offers books from many publishers and several countries.

Charles and Co.
823 11th Ave.
New York, NY 10019-3535
This firm operates a fresh-cut "Flowers of the Month" club, for 3, 6, or 12 months.

Condor Farms, Inc.
1800 N.W. 89th Place
Miami, FL 33172
Condor Farms is a major wholesale distributor of fresh flowers imported from Central and South America. Sterling Bouquet, a sister firm in Miami, makes thousands of bouquets for U.S. supermarkets. Wholesale buyers may contact Condor for further information.

T. DeBaggio Lavender
923 N. Ivy St.
Arlington, VA 22201
This firm is a grower of several types of lavender and rosemary. They will ship plants via mail in spring season.

Floral Resources/Hawaii, Inc.
175 E. Kawailani St.
Hilo, HI 96720
Grower and wholesale shipper of tropical orchids, anthuriums, proteas, orchids, and exotic foliage. Floral Resources is a major distributor of crops grown at Costa Flores in Costa Rica, a plantation seen in chapter 3.

Johnny's Selected Seeds
Foss Hill Road
Albion, ME 04910
The firm offers seeds of flowers and vegetables, some growing supplies. Flowers good for cutting are marked with a "clippers" symbol in the catalog listing.

Logee's Greenhouses
55 North St.
Danielson, CT 06239
The color illustrated catalog offers many flowering indoor plants, ferns, and herbs.

Maxima Farms, Inc.
1411 N.W. 89th Court
Miami, FL 33172
This Colombian company grows and ships premium grade Maxima Farms carnations and newly developed Germini miniature gerberas. Wholesale buyers may contact them for information about their Colombian-grown flowers.

Rod McLellan Co.
1450 El Camino Real
South San Francisco, CA 94080
A specialist in orchid plants, the firm also ships preserved eucalyptus and some flower-arranging supplies. A local shop offers fresh-cut flowers and containers.

Ohio Florists' Association
2130 Stella Court
Columbus, OH 43215
This organization sponsors the yearly International Floriculture Short Course and sells several publications related to the floriculture industry. Write directly for information on the course or publications.

Orchids only!
P.O. Box 915
Medford, OR 97501

This division of Harry and David Company, the famous shippers of gourmet fruit, offers premium cut orchids. Free color folders are issued at major holidays. Their cymbidiums are U.S. grown; arandas and dendrobiums are imported from Singapore.

George W. Park Seed Co.
Box 31
Greenwood, SC 29647-0001
The free catalog lists some flower-arranging supplies, plus many seeds and plants for growing your own fresh flowers.

Protea Farms of California
P.O. Box 1806
Fallbrook, CA 92028
This grower offers fresh protea family flowers including unusual banksias, leucodendrons, and leucospermums. Free price list.

Protea Gardens of Maui
RR 2 Box 389
Kula, HI 96790
The company grows and ships proteas, banksias, and other tropical foliage and flowers. They will sell and ship retail orders and make bouquets for gifts; the firm also offers dry proteas and similar tropicals.

Rainbow Tropicals
P.O. Box 4038
Hilo, HI 96720
The firm offers direct retail express shipments of Hawaiian-grown fresh flowers and some potted flowering plants. Write for a free list.

Shepherd's Garden Seeds
30 Irene St.
Torrington, CT 06790

This firm sells many old-fashioned flowers good for bouquets and drying. The catalog includes broad selections of vegetables and herbs, some of which also look nice in arrangements.

Smith & Hawken
25 Corte Madera
Mill Valley, CA 94941
Write for a free catalog of arranging supplies, some plants, garden supplies, books, and cut flowers by mail.

Thompson & Morgan
P.O. Box 1308
Jackson, NJ 08527
This company has an excellent selection of seeds and offers many flowers good for cutting. The catalog is well illustrated.

Wayside Gardens
1 Garden Lane
Hodges, SC 29695-0001
This well-known company has an outstanding catalog of flowering and foliage plants, many useful in arrangements.

White Flower Farm
Litchfield, CT 06759-0050
The catalog offers containers, flowering bulbs, and some indoor plants, plus many hardy garden plants. Some plants and fresh wreaths are offered at holiday times. Selections especially appropriate as cut flowers are so noted in the catalog.

Winterthur Museum and Gardens
100 Enterprise Place
Dover, DE 19901
The free catalog includes unusual containers for cut flowers.

Further Reading

American Plant Life Society. *Proceedings: International Symposium on Bulbous and Cormous Plants.* National City, Calif.: Herbertia Journal, vol. 45, 1989.
This collection of research papers is useful for readers interested in plant breeding and commercial cut-flower growing.

Association of Specialty Cut Flower Growers. *Proceedings of 2d National Conference on Specialty Cut Flowers.* Athens, Ga.: Department of Horticulture, University of Georgia, 1989.
Research findings and growing suggestions presented by professionals for growers of unusual cut flowers.

Ball, Geo. J., Co. *Grower Talks.* Geneva, Ill.: Monthly.
Grower Talks is a magazine for commercial growers. Articles frequently include new reasearch results and reports on recent flower introductions.

Berry, Fred, and W. John Kress. *Heliconia: An Identification Guide.* Washington: Smithsonian Institution Press, 1991.
This useful guide by two international authorities shows 200 heliconias in full color. The taxonomic notes are helpful in getting names correct when ordering heliconia flowers. Plants are grouped as having an erect or pendent inflorescence, a useful division for flower arrangers.

Chen, Youngkan Y. K., ed. *Flowers from Taiwan.* Taipei: Taiwan Floriculture Development Association, 1990.
Useful paperback book showing most of the cut-flower and pot-plant crops grown in the Republic of China. Symbols indicate seasonal availability of the crops shown.

Ferguson, J. Barry, and Tom Cowan. *Living with Flowers.* New York: Rizzoli International Publications, 1990.
Suggestions for choosing, arranging, and giving flowers presented by a talented flower designer. Lovely photographs showing flower displays in party settings and spacious homes.

Fitch, Charles Marden. *All About Orchids.* New York: Doubleday, 1981.
How to grow tropical orchids; section on corsages.

————. *The Complete Book of Houseplants.* New York: Hawthorn Books, 1972.
How to grow and enjoy tropical plants. Many photographs of plants suitable for arrangements with cut flowers.

————. *The Complete Book of Miniature Roses.* New York: Hawthorn Books, 1977.
Growing and showing miniature roses. Section on growing plants indoors, history of miniature roses.

Florists' Review. Topeka, Kans.: Florists' Review Enterprises.
Professionally oriented monthly magazine for florists. Annual sourcebook lists sources of flowers, foliage, supplies, and addresses for florist organizations.

Flower Council of Holland. *Cut Flowers.* Leiden, Holland: Bloemen Bureau Holland, 1990.
Florists rely on this small but colorful book to choose among more than 600 of the favorite cut flowers sold at the famous Dutch auctions. Symbols and an introduction in 6 languages make this a useful international guide.

Hawaii Department of Agriculture. *Hawaii's Floral and Nursery Products.* Honolulu: Hawaii Department of Agriculture, Market Development Branch, 1991.
This informative paperback book lists Hawaiian flower and plant exporters. Exporters are grouped according to products available. Charts show seasonal availability of flowers from Hawaii. Color photographs illustrate some of the most popular types.

Healey, Deryck. *The New Art of Flower Design.* New York: Villard Books, 1986.
Arrangements to suit varied settings and occasions created by a talented English designer. Well illustrated with beautiful photographs.

Hillier, Malcolm. *The Book of Fresh Flowers.* New York: Simon and Schuster, 1988.
Beautiful photographs of live materials and large arrangements in the English style.

Holstead, Christy L. *Care and Handling of Flowers and Plants Manual.* Alexandria, Va.: Society of American Florists, 1985.
A loose-leaf manual providing useful flower care instructions written by a manager of Floralife, with contributions from various specialists in the flower trade.

Ikenobo, Senei. *Ikebana of Senei Ikenobo Free Style.* Tokyo, Japan: Shufunotomo, 1980.
Twenty bold designs of flowers with foliage.

International Bulb Society. *Herbertia.* Irvine, Ca.: International Bulb Society. Yearly journal.
Contributions to this color-illustrated journal offer advanced information about bulbous plants including trends in hybridizing cut-flower types.

Jacobs, Betty E. M. *Flowers That Last Forever.* Pownal, Vt.: Storey Communications, 1988.
Practical approach to growing and preserving flowers that are attractive when dried.

Mitchell, Herb, ed. *Design with Flowers* magazine. Costa Mesa, Calif.: Herb Mitchell Associates. Five times per year.
A large-format magazine aimed at professional designers. Photographs and text offer designers inspiring ideas. The spring issue concentrates on ways to use fresh flowers at weddings.

Okada, Kozan. *Ikebana with the Seasons.* Tokyo, Japan: Shufunotomo, 1989.
Striking photographs of traditional and modern ikebana arrangements. Wild and cultivated flowers are combined with branches or grasses according to the seasons.

Pokon and Chrysal. *Everything About Caring for Fresh Flowers.* Naarden, Holland: Pokon and Chrysal, 1990.
This 11-page booklet outlines basic cut-flower care and provides details about the 5 Chrysal preservative formulas. Some florists and supermarket flower counters offer free copies of this useful pamphlet.

Riffin, Lisa. *Leonard Tharp: An American Style in Flower Arrangement.* Dallas: Taylor Publishing, 1986.
Unusual ideas for blending vegetables, grasses, and other ingredients in fresh flower displays. Unique designs for large spaces.

Royal Horticultural Society. *The Garden.* London: The Royal Horticultural Society, and Home and Law Publisher.
Monthly magazine for gardeners with occasional articles about using fresh flowers indoors.

Sacalis, John N. *Fresh Cut Flowers for Designs.* Columbus, Ohio: D. C. Kiplinger Chair in Floriculture, Ohio State University, 1989.
This paperback volume is one of several guides prepared under the leadership of Dr. Henry M. Cathey, when he was director of the United States National Arboretum. The book cites recent research findings for postproduction care of more than 40 genera.

Teleflora. *Flowers&.* Los Angeles, Calif.: Teleflora. Monthly.
A magazine for professionals in the floral business. Good ideas for florists and designers presented by the international wire service company Teleflora.

United States Department of Agriculture. *Wholesale Ornamental Crops Reports.* Various cities and states: U.S.D.A. Marketing Service and state agricultural departments.
The U.S.D.A. and local state agricultural departments join in publishing these timely reports twice weekly, covering data from major wholesale markets including those in California, Florida, Hawaii, New York, and Pennsylvania. Fresh flower reports mention quantities sold, source of fresh flowers, prices received in relation to quality or grades, and demand/availability data.

Vaughan, Mary Jane. *The Complete Book of Cut Flower Care.* Portland, Oreg.: Timber Press, 1988.
Practical suggestions by a commercial flower grower and florist.

Viveiros, Henry, ed. *The Flower Market.* San Jose, Calif.: Henry Viveiros.
A monthly newspaper for professionals in the fresh flower business. Features on growing, marketing, and research findings.

Webb, Iris, ed. *The Complete Guide to Flower and Foliage Arrangement.* New York: Doubleday, 1979.
A dozen contributors cover many styles of flower arranging. Chapters include in-depth information of design categories, exhibition work, and ikebana.

Index

(Page numbers in *italic* refer to illustrations.)

254

Acknowledgments

Gathering information on location around the world is exciting, but the hard work can be exhausting without the help of people where flowers are grown. Thank you to all of my friends who assisted with my location research and answered countless questions with friendly patience. Especially helpful with this book were Kun Somsak and Kun Thonglor in Thailand, Michael Ooi in Malaysia, Irawati in Indonesia, Zhang Li in the People's Republic of China, Captain Claude Hope and David Carli in Costa Rica, Roland Iguina and associates at Hawaiian Cut Flowers in New York City, Lorraine Roxbury of Grant's Florist in Larchmont, New York, Russ Miller at *Grower Talks* magazine, Eleanor Clevenger of Creative Resources in Miami, Dora Galitzki, Dr. Rupert C. Barneby, and the library staff at the New York Botanical Garden. A special thanks to friends at Abbeville Press, including my enthusiastic editor Susan Costello, talented designer Nai Y. Chang, and efficient production supervisor Hope Koturo.

During my research in many countries people have shared their knowledge and cultures. Their much-appreciated international assistance greatly enriches *Fresh Flowers*.